PRAISE FOR LUCI GABEL'S EAT TO LEAD

I love this book, it's like having a coach by your side. It's as if Luci's talking directly to me, I can feel her encouragement and hear her enthusiasm!

—Robin Tucker, LPC, Psychotherapist & Leadership Coach

Ancient Greeks believed that a "sound mind in a sound body" was one of the virtuous things a person should strive to achieve. *Eat to Lead* is a key step in Luci's Way—combining the physical and mental readiness that serve as the foundation for modern-day leadership. The accelerating rate of change and the increasing complexity of today's world place stresses on executives and other leaders unmatched in recent— or any— historical flow of events. An effective leader knows to take care of both body and mind, the key tools in maintaining energy and effectiveness. This book offers a lucid and workable way of doing just that. If you look at today's leaders, men and women alike, it is obvious who is healthy and vigorous and who is not. Despite stage-managed appearances and sound bites, long term activity and accomplishments tell the story of who is fit to lead. It could be you.

—Jack N. Cole, Ph.D., Jack N. Cole Consulting: Intelligent Strategies for Navigating the Information Environment

D0910348

Transformational Leadership—the kind that creates breakthrough engagement and enthusiasm requires internal reflection, devotion to your personal vitality and health as well as communication tools that land. Luci's book and her methodology tells you how you can use easy, timely and quick practices to build your leadership and start feeling energized, clear minded and unstoppable in your day-to-day life whilst creating a team environment that is genuinely exciting to be a part of.

—Sunil Bhaskaran, Founder, Global Business Mastermind

This book by smart nutritionist Luci Gabel guides you in making your own personal food decisions that lead to higher energy levels, more brainpower, better sleep, weight loss, disease prevention, and more. The pace is designed to fit into the life of a busy professional.

—Lee Constantine, Co-founder, Publishizer.com

EAT TO LEAD

Luci Gabel

atmosphere press

TABLE OF CONTENTS

| INTRODUCTION |
HOW TO GET THE MOST OUT OF THIS BOOK

You can be a leader in many ways and places: in your work, in your family, in social groups, or in communities large and small. Most of us aren't leaders in every aspect of life, but we take on leadership in the right circumstances. Some of us choose to be leaders, others fall into the role.

One thing is certain—we aren't automatically a leader because we're appointed to a position or given a title. A true leader is someone who people want to follow. Make no mistake, this is the kind of leader I'm referring to throughout this book.

To the extent that characteristics of leaders have been studied, we know that we choose to follow leaders who share our values and goals. We follow leaders because they give us hope for a positive future. We look to leaders for guidance and support. We want our leaders to make good decisions and be a good example. Most importantly, we follow leaders who inspire us.

Leaders who inspire are almost always connected to a big vision of a better future, and they communicate their vision well. They're clear about their values and are bold enough to live by them even when it's difficult. They're self-motivated and motivate others. They think creatively and innovate. They have good people skills. All of this takes time and energy to develop and refine.

Most people aren't born with leadership skills. But these are skills that can be learned and improved with time and practice. The best leaders are the first to admit their imperfections, and they work on themselves continuously. They read, attend classes, hire mentors and coaches. They

3

aren't afraid to ask for help when it's needed. The most successful leaders are always working to learn and grow both personally and professionally, much like you are now as you read this book.

No doubt, at some point you figured out that leadership not only takes skill, it takes energy and stamina. You may have entertained the idea that eating the right foods could help you have the mental and physical power, endurance, and resilience to be the best leader you can possibly be. If so, you were right! Food can energize, fortify, and sustain you for all the activities you take on in your leadership roles, and all the other activities you want to enjoy.

Although eating is something we all do, eating in the right way isn't a skill set we're born with either. For many of us, it's also not a skill set we were taught while growing up. But it is not difficult and does not have to be time-consuming—it can fit into a full and satisfying leadership life. In fact, if you want to be the best leader you can be, you need to know how to eat right. It is not a luxury, it's a necessity.

Research shows that what you eat not only affects the shape of your body, it affects the structure of your brain. We know now that eating the right foods can even influence your DNA to look and perform like a younger version of itself. In fact, the right food choices can help you look, feel, and perform, as if you were 10 to 15 years younger. With a stronger, healthier body and mind from better food choices, you'll be well-positioned to be a better leader. On your journey through this book I'll share how all of this is possible. If you decide to make some of the changes to your food choices that I suggest, you'll be laying a strong foundation for excellent physical and mental health and performance, now and far into the future. You'll be more productive and effective in leadership and everything else you do.

If you have the slightest worry that putting a little more time or energy into taking better care of yourself could be selfish, I assure you it's not. If you want to improve your performance at work, be more creative and make better decisions long into the evening, you'll benefit from choosing food that enables you to start your day strong and have long-term, even-keeled energy. If you're interested in taking better care of others, including those you lead and those you love, you'll benefit from food choices that help you to stay attentive and focused, and sustain better moods. Of course, if you want to feel and look your best, eating the right food will definitely help. Consequently, the right food choices can help you to have more confidence, move up a corporate ladder, be a better people-person, even help you make more money if you so desire. The right food choices will support you in being a stronger, more competent, and capable individual with more to offer everyone.

Because you're busy, you can't afford to waste time or energy changing your diet if it doesn't ultimately get you to your goals. Above all, it should help you to feel, think and perform your best for a lifetime. For this reason, you need to avoid wasting time and energy on fads—and there are so many of them. You need to avoid the confusion perpetuated by all kinds of media. You also need a food plan that fits into your lifestyle and your schedule, and one that works with your body. I'll help you with that. And I'll debunk some of the most popular fads and clear up some confusion as you learn how food works with your body.

Don't Settle

Leaders are generally not the kind of people who settle for average results. Because you're reading this, I'm willing to bet you strive to be better than average in work and life. Along with that, you probably want to be the healthiest version of yourself and enjoy life to the fullest for the longest time possible. You don't want to just live; you want to thrive! And you can.

It doesn't matter how old you are. I've worked with

hundreds of people at all stages of life and I've seen what's possible as we age. It can be unexpectedly great if we do it right. In fact, it's possible for you to live a healthier, more vibrant, vital life than you ever imagined. You can also be a relevant and valuable leader with a strong and capable mind and body, much further into the future than you may have thought you would. That is provided you (a) know how to take the best care of yourself, and (b) put your knowledge into action daily.

My Story

I've had numerous experiences with leadership in my life so far. Shortly after college I became the director of a health club and spa in Seoul, South Korea. It was a morale, welfare, and recreation Department of Defense facility for the U.S. military in Asia. I grew what was at first a small spa and fitness center into a full-service health club, with a staff of 90 people and seven departments, which was frequented by generals and other high-profile guests. We offered the highest quality service with the greatest attention to detail. Before I left, I was honored with the Commander's Award for Civilian Service for my work.

Afterward, I served as manager at a prestigious health club and spa in Honolulu, Hawaii, where I increased the revenue and profits of my department in the short time period that I spent there. Later, I became a start-up founder in a company launching a boutique fitness club and spa in Washington, D.C. I was integral in the decision-making and development of the entire facility. It was a place that attracted government officials, diplomats, TV personalities, journalists, and well-known members of the D.C. social scene. By the time I left, it had received significant attention from the press as well as industry awards for innovation and quality. In all of these positions, I had the responsibility of leading a wide range of skilled professionals through organizational growth and change, while maintaining the highest quality of services for customers. To be successful, I couldn't just be a manager or an owner, I needed to be the best leader I possibly could be.

Now, I'm an entrepreneur with a business of my own that's been through several successful stages of change. I work with private and corporate clients across the country and educate an international audience online. At this point in time I've held positions of leadership, I've worked alongside leaders, and I've groomed leaders too—I'm familiar with the challenges that leadership brings.

I Wasn't Born with It

Throughout my career, I continued to work with clients one-on-one and in groups whenever time permitted. As a result, I've helped hundreds of people to improve their performance, health, and lives. Many have been leaders: entrepreneurs, CEOs, competitive athletes, military officers, even royalty. Many clients I've worked with achieved greater health, vitality, and energy than they thought possible. Some of my clients in their fifties, sixties, and seventies have confessed that because of our work, they feel and perform better than they did in their twenties.

I, too, feel and perform better than I did in my twenties. When people see me in person, observe my physique and energy, and hear what I do for a living, most assume I had an extremely healthy upbringing, I'm gifted genetically, or that I spend hours in the gym and have an extremely restrictive diet. But none of these are the case.

My family is like most families in America. We don't have the genetics that allows us to eat anything we want and stay thin. I don't come from a lineage of Olympians or professional athletes. While growing up, my family didn't have dinnertime chats about how food affects our energy, health, and longevity. It was beyond our scope of knowledge that food could influence our mental capacity. In fact, my dad supported a family of five on a graduate-school stipend for many years, so we ate from boxes and cans most of the time. Like many American families, our focus was on eating hearty and eating enough. And like many teen girls, I learned about diet mostly from magazines and television.

My grandmothers loved making dinners for others and enjoyed hosting large groups on holidays. Most likely because of their great cooking I've always liked eating. But I wasn't drawn to making meals, nor was I fond of spending time in the kitchen except when visiting them.

I became interested in health during college and entered the premedicine program with concentrations in both psychology and physiology. Once finished, I decided not to pursue medical school. I had discovered how miraculous the human body is, and how well it thrives when we take care of it the right way. I became more interested in prevention than medicine.

I paid my way through college as an exercise instructor, and while deciding what to do next I worked as a certified personal trainer in Manhattan. I also entered the modeling industry and learned the diet most popular there at the time— semi-starvation. It was definitely not going to be my long-term option. You'll see shortly how my education and experience in health and diet up to that point was not enough for me to know how to obtain the health, energy, and stamina that I needed for leadership.

The Struggle Is Real

I was determined to stay in excellent physical condition from the start of my career. While holding leadership positions I got my black belt in Taekwondo, received instructor training in Pilates and yoga, and competed in triathlons and other endurance events. But with all the exercise I was doing, my body didn't look the way I thought it should. I didn't sleep well or fall asleep easily at night, despite how tired I was. Sometimes I'd fight painful migraines that forced me to pace the floor in the middle of the night because lying down wasn't an option. I came down with serious illnesses that seemed to come out of nowhere and would put me in bed for days. I was performing well, and it looked like I had it all together from the outside, but I was struggling behind the scenes.

I sought help from other health professionals. Some told me I was lactose intolerant, so I avoided dairy. Others told me I was gluten intolerant, so I stopped eating wheat. I avoided red meat and eggs because of their alleged harm to my health. I tried food combining, not eating past certain times of the evening, and many other popular trends that sent me searching through specialty grocery stores for my prescribed food and supplements.

I was hoping to figure out how food could provide me with more energy, better mental focus and acuity, a stronger immune system, and, ideally, make me more attractive. I didn't find that on my quest. I did, however, find myself lacking in food choices when eating with friends and family. I was perpetually tired and hungry, and I went through energy highs and lows that I couldn't figure out. Eventually, I tried all the most popular diets with no success in finding one that would support my ideal weight and health and give me the energy I wanted and needed. Then, everything changed.

I returned to school to study nutrition. My end goal was to understand diets for myself and then help others do the same. The four-year nutrition and dietetics degree program took me through all the sciences—microbiology, biology, biochemistry, physics, genetics—you name it. All of these topics play a part in understanding how the body works in conjunction with food. We even had a few courses on the chemistry of cooking and how to run a restaurant kitchen. I signed up for the nutrition program because I wanted to study diets, and to my initial frustration, there was no mention of diets until the fourth year! As it turns out, that was a good thing, because I had been approaching food and eating the wrong way. Eventually I learned how to make food decisions based on science, not based on what diets make the headlines.

I started incorporating my education into my own life from day one. But it took years of keeping up with current research, practicing my knowledge on myself and working with others, to really grasp the subtleties of nutrition and how it works in conjunction with life. After finishing nutrition studies at the University of Maryland, College Park, I went on to get my master's in exercise physiology there while pursuing my MBA at Johns Hopkins. It was only after finishing an advanced education in the human body that I was able use nutrition to benefit my work and leadership in the way I'd always wanted.

Today I'm like most who own a business or run a corporation; I wear many hats and juggle it all. And like most, I feel there's never enough time in my day to get it all done. But now I create time for new experiences, meaningful relationships, and regular travel. I maintain high levels of energy and stamina throughout long workdays, I sleep well at night, I've rid myself of headaches, and I rarely get sick. I also enjoy a level of fitness that many feel is impossible for themselves with the number of responsibilities they juggle. But it is possible for you. And I intend for you start experiencing this kind of energy, health, and stamina for yourself as we move forward.

The undeniable fact is, food plays a major supporting role in my ability to live the kind of life I desire and be the person I want to be. Food has many purposes: it is a fuel, it's a source of pleasure, it's a reason to gather with people, it's an integral part of history and traditions, and it's a tool that can be used to improve your performance in life and leadership—provided you know how. I wrote this book so you can benefit from my life's work and experiences, and so you can perform at your best and do what you love for years to come. Food can and will support you in the big, satisfying life you want to live.

The Only Way to Eat Right: Make It Personal

Nutrition science evolves. Contrary to popular belief, it doesn't change so fast that we can't keep up, nor does it swing back and forth like a pendulum in terms of what scientists agree on. But media and popular trends make it look that way.

My education was based on science, and I've continued to keep abreast of nutrition science as it moves along. I'll share a secret with you: popular media frequently misinterprets nutrition science. To clarify, when I say media, I mean the news, magazines, and social media, as well as TV, movies, and even some books. I'm not saying they all do it intentionally, but let's face it—understanding scientific research is hard to do without training; if someone isn't trained in the fundamentals it will be difficult for them to correctly interpret the research.

As misinformation about nutrition gets passed around, it can create widespread, long-lasting, and often very lucrative fads. Anyone can be a victim of this misinformation—even health professionals—if they don't take the time to review the research for themselves. As a result, I've seen far too many people struggling, choosing diets that don't serve them, wasting their valuable time and energy making habit changes over and over again because popular media has misled them. It saddens me.

Clients and friends have suggested I write a diet book. But I can't do that. Because everyone has different bodies, lifestyles, activity levels, food preferences, and digestive systems, all of which require slightly different ways of eating to feel and be optimal. Throughout my career, I've helped clients learn about their own bodies and the fundamentals of how food works and then put the two together in a way that uniquely fits their life. I can't see it working any other way.

Therefore, this book isn't a diet program with specific menus and times to eat. I won't give you lists of foods to strictly avoid. I won't lead you into the latest diet craze, or make you eat ad nauseam the "superfood" that's in fashion this year. The information I'll share is based on current, scientific knowledge in nutrition and physiology and the accumulation of my experience. This book is meant to be your personal, transformational journey with food that lasts a lifetime.

Because I know you're busy, I'll share information as concisely as possible, so you can take what you need and move forward. You can do a deeper dive into the subjects through resources in the reference section at the end. If you'd like more help from me on improving your food choices or your leadership life overall, you'll find my coaching and group programs at EatToLead.com. Before moving on, I'd like to share a little about what is in the book and why.

Let's Optimize Your Brain Power

Approximately 20% of the energy you spend daily is attributed to brain activity. That's a lot of energy if you think about how small your brain is compared to your body! Research in neuroscience finds that the most energy-demanding activities of the brain are conscious activities—those that are not habitual and require thought. David Rock, author of *Your Brain at Work*, explains that the majority of conscious activities can be grouped into five categories:

1) memorizing
2) understanding (synthesizing or decoding information)
3) deciding
4) recalling
5) inhibiting (also known as restraint, or willpower)

These activities are performed by the prefrontal cortex part of your brain, appropriately called the executive functioning area. As a leader, you're using the executive functioning area of your brain, performing one or more of these energy-hungry activities constantly.

Neuroscience today also finds there's a limit to the number of these activities that we can perform well every day. For example, once one decision is made, we have less energy and fuel to make the next. Our brain, like the body, gets depleted. It needs regular fuel, and eventually sleep, to continue performing at its best. The funny thing is that we wouldn't think to exercise our body intensely all day and into the night without food, water, and rest. But we ask our brains to perform that way without thinking twice. And then we wonder why we get so tired after making decisions all day!

David Rock therefore recommends we do our most demanding mental tasks and make our most important decisions when our brain is fresh and alert. One of the best times for this, he says, is first thing in the morning when our brain is rested and we have plenty of fuel to access.

Decisions about food also use our executive functioning energy. You may not notice it, but with each decision you inevitably need to:

- Recall whether you've eaten the food before and if you want to eat it again.

- Understand what the food is made of if you haven't eaten it before.

- Decide whether or not you'll eat it based on the information you have.

- Resist urges to eat the less-healthy foods you may be craving.

If you're planning to eat with a group or trying to fit a meal into a busy day, you need to spend additional mental energy. All of this is energy that your brain could use for other, more complex and challenging decisions. Many leaders, either consciously or subconsciously, decide not to spend energy on decisions about food. Many grab whatever food is available or skip eating altogether. You'll soon find out how avoiding decisions about food and skipping meals can cause even bigger problems down the road.

You Need a System

Well-run businesses have systems to repeat processes that work, so they don't have to spend needless energy figuring out how to be successful at something over and over again. Brendon Burchard, author of *High Performance Habits* and founder of the High Performance Institute, discovered that high-performing individuals have systems not only for work but also for life. Systems can be created for everything, from how you pick out your clothes in the morning to how you prepare for meetings in the afternoon. The more systems you have in place for daily, routine tasks, the more mental energy you spare for all of your other, more mentally demanding activities.

Personal systems are one of the secrets to how high performers achieve above and beyond what most others can, in less time than most others can. You can have your own systems for success. They can make you faster and more efficient at everything, and help you excel in leadership as well as life.

You can also have systems for food. The people I've worked with who've been most successful at eating for optimal performance and health were those who had systems for it. The best part is, you can set up your system so that it not only ensures you have energy to power through your day but also provides you with the nutrients necessary to support a high-quality, long-lasting, and fabulous life. Of course, you need to devote some brain power and put a little energy into creating a system. Everyone does. But a small effort now pays off big later.

My System Is Now Yours

Within the following chapters I've inserted a series of steps to help you create a personal food system that works for you, and that you enjoy. Starting from the foundation of your current habits, I'll help you to make more beneficial food choices that uniquely work with your body and life and support you in being a true leader—someone who people want to follow. The knowledge and skills you acquire here will enable you to adjust and refine your system as you go, so it gets better over time.

It's well known that small, consistent steps are the easiest way to succeed at making lasting dietary habit changes. So, the individual steps I suggest are small and will add up to a giant positive leap forward for you and your food choices in the end. If you take consistent action, in as little as six weeks you can have a personalized system that enables you to easily eat for more energy, helps you feel and look your best, and supports your productivity and creativity, good moods, mental focus, and health and longevity.

The steps are in a specific order for a reason: those that will give you the most profound results are at the beginning to jump-start your progress. The nutrition information builds on itself and will make more sense as you continue reading. Just like climbing to a mountain's peak, simply put one foot in front of the other until you reach the top; for best results proceed in order and read the whole book. If for some reason you aren't able to take the steps I suggest, reading the book is better than nothing. If that's the case, I hope you can come back and take the steps another time.

Just like we can see different views from the top of a mountain depending on where we stand, everyone taking these steps will have different outcomes based on where they stand with food. Your results will depend not only on your physiology but also on your schedule, lifestyle, and energy needs. The information here is flexible and versatile: if you read this book again a year from now, you might experience it completely differently.

Since common knowledge isn't always common practice, you may be familiar with some of the concepts I talk about, but you may not be putting your knowledge into practice. If that's the case you're not alone. One phrase I regularly hear from people is, "I know what to do, but I'm just not doing it." If this is true for you, I'd like to help you put an end to that. Read on to find out how.

Maximize Your Opportunity for Success

Research has found that we can learn faster and remember more if we engage in a variety of activities related to what we're learning. This solidifies our learning by spreading it throughout multiple areas of our brain. If you want to make habit changes fast and make them last, bring what you read here into as many areas of your life as you can, as soon as you can. For the most successful transformation in short order, here's what I suggest:

1. Read a chapter per week and take action on what you learn immediately. Give yourself at least a week to practice the corresponding dietary changes before moving on. That's enough time for you to gain solid footing on a habit change but not enough time to lose momentum.

2. Share what you learn and share your goals. Goals that are shared are more likely to be achieved because it introduces the element of accountability; when others know what you're up to, it increases your motivation to follow through. Even better, invite someone to join you on your food journey; research finds that social support is a big factor in successfully changing food habits.

3. Journal as you go. You're going to make some discoveries about yourself and food that you'll want to remember. And yet, if you're like most of my clients, you won't remember your discoveries two weeks down the road without documentation—because life is busy!

There's evidence that handwriting on paper reinforces the memory best. To make writing convenient for you, I've put journal pages in the Dynamic Lifestyle Road Map™ at the back of the book. If you don't want to write by hand, type notes on your preferred device. The important thing is that you document your experience for this short time in order to get the most out of it.

The Dynamic Lifestyle Road Map™

As you know reading isn't the same as making changes in real life. The Dynamic Lifestyle Road Map in the second half of this book is your first step in turning these words on a page into your life experiences. I'll guide you in documenting your food journey, and making useful conclusions and decisions based on your notes. This is the only way to create a food plan that works for your unique life. As a bonus, you'll be inadvertently tracking your progress, which will make all your improvements and successes much more obvious—and easier to celebrate!

Let's Make These Changes Stick

Our personal desires and aspirations are our most profound motivators. When the going gets tough, it's our desires, dreams, and even the fears closest to our hearts that drive us forward despite difficulty or challenges. As leaders, we are powerful motivators when we help others to see that avoiding their worst fear is possible and turning their goals and dreams into reality is achievable. Likewise, as a leader, your own big motivators need to be in the forefront of your mind so you can access them when you need motivation to keep moving forward. These motivators are often referred to as our "Big Why."

What's your "Big Why" for reading this book? Only you know the most important reasons why you want to change your eating habits for the better. Maybe you desire the long-term health, energy, and vitality that eating the right foods can provide, so you can feel and look your best while pursuing your highest goals. Maybe you want to improve your physical and mental stamina so you can perform optimally during the long hours you keep. Or, maybe you'd like to avoid the health issues that tend to show up with age, so you can continue to be a vital contribution to the world long into the future. These are some of the most popular reasons why people with a leadership mindset make changes to their eating habits. Yours will be unique and powerful drivers behind your own personal success.

Now, Get Clear on Your "Why"

Before closing the book, go to the Dynamic Lifestyle Road Map and get a solid start by writing down your "Big Why" for reading this book and wanting to create healthier eating habits. Go deep. Be honest. Write down not only how changing your food habits for the better will benefit you but also how this change can impact those around you—from colleagues to team members, to people you lead, family and friends, your community, even the world. Keep your "Big Why" in the forefront of your mind as you continue reading and taking steps to change your food choices.

Congratulations on getting started! The sooner you begin to make better food choices, the sooner you'll start feeling and seeing the benefits, and it only gets better with time. I know it's not easy to commit to something new when you already have so much on your plate. But there's significant value in it. The value will likely be greater than you expect and have longer-term, more positive effects than you can even foresee at this time.

You deserve all the energy and benefits that food can offer, and you deserve to enjoy it too! In the next chapter, we'll build a solid foundation to support your success now and long into the future as you *Eat to Lead*.

| CHAPTER 1 |
DECISION-MAKING SKILLS AND STARTING OFF STRONG

First, let me acknowledge you because you've decided to take action and make changes that benefit your leadership and life. Your efforts to improve your food choices can have a profound and positive impact not only on yourself but also on those you lead and influence and those you love. Evidence for this will reveal itself as you progress through this book, especially if you take action on what you learn. For now, keep in mind that your decision to make healthy changes to your food choices is a good one, and your willingness to look at your habits and make changes for the better is a strong characteristic of a good leader.

Decision-Making

Out of all the responsibilities leaders have, decision-making is one of the biggest. Leaders make all kinds of decisions, large and small, every day. Let's be honest, decision-making is not only an energy-demanding process, but it's also a weighty one; the decisions we make shape the way people see us as a leader.

Carol O'Connor, author of *Secrets of Great Leaders*, explains that people don't expect leaders to have a crystal ball. They do, however, want them to make an effort to get all the facts necessary to make the best decision possible. She says if followers know you did your best with the information and data available, you can keep their respect even if a decision fails. I'll take it a step further and say that if people respect you and also have a history of trust and positive experiences with you, it'll be easy for them to stick with you through many challenges. Your leadership can be long-lasting, if you want it to be!

Initial Data

Whether a decision is about leadership, food, or anything else, it's clear that data is extremely helpful when it comes to making the best decisions. When we're about to make any change, gathering the initial data (also called baseline data) is the only way we can objectively see where we are now, what kind of change is needed, and whether a change is even needed in the first place. After making a change, we can look back at our baseline data as a reference to see if our decision has gotten us closer to our goals or if we need to do something different. Without initial data, we're just guessing about progress and whether our decision had the impact we wanted.

We can use data from surveys, market testing, financial reports, online reviews, and personal observations to help in our decision-making. But leaders go one step further: they talk to the people who will be affected by their decisions and listen with open ears.

Exceptional Leaders Listen

Listening gives you the pulse of the group you're hoping to influence, whether it's your team, your customers, your family, or your fans. Listening also helps people to like and trust you. At the very least, it earns respect.

In their study of more than 300,000 business leaders, Jack Zenger and Joseph Folkman found that the most successful leaders around the world are highly skilled at building relationships and trust. But there's a popular misconception that building relationships and trust involves talking— explaining our thoughts, goals, missions, and plans. While it's important as a leader to be a good communicator, it's even more important to listen well and actually hear what people are saying. Listening to the perspectives of the people you lead provides priceless data that helps you make the best decisions for the group. Additionally, it helps people feel included in the decision-making and ultimately helps them be more comfortable with a decision.

Building Trust and Relationship

Everyone values being heard. It's such a fundamental need that it's been woven through the fiber of our neurology. A brain scan study at the University of California, Santa Barbara, found that talking about oneself releases dopamine. It makes people feel just as good as if they ate some chocolate or played with a puppy! Yet, in our technological world where people's attention is constantly divided, it can feel like a rare gift when someone not only hears you but pays attention to what you're saying and remembers it. A great leader leaves people feeling like what they have to say is important and that they've been heard. Over and above data gathering, good listening creates an atmosphere of trust and cultivates positive relationships.

Good listening skills require only a little practice to develop. The next time you're in a conversation with anyone, whether it's someone you work with, a colleague, a family member, or a friend, notice whether you're genuinely listening and hearing what they're saying or whether you're going off on tangents in your mind and losing track of what they're saying. If listening well is difficult for you, it's worth practicing and improving on it. An excellent practice in effective listening is to repeat back to the speaker some of the most notable points they made in the conversation. This reinforces your understanding of what's been said, solidifies your memory of the discussion, and assures the speaker they've been heard. For example, you can start by saying, "Let me be sure I understand what you're saying," and proceed from there.

Listening as part of your data is particularly important before leading people through a change. People are much more willing to be led through change by someone that they respect, like, and trust. Similarly, collecting information about food—including listening to your body's reactions, signs, and signals—will help you trust that you're making the right food choices. In fact, getting better at this kind of introspective listening will strengthen your trust in your own decisions about leadership and life overall. We'll explore this further in upcoming pages.

What and Why

Leaders gather initial data to make decisions regarding change. Once we figure out what changes need to be made, we set goals and decide on the smaller steps we'll take to achieve them. After getting started, we evaluate our progress along the way and make modifications as needed. This is how we successfully change the course of an organization; it's also how we successfully change habits as individuals.

Naturally then, your first step is to get initial data on your current food habits. Then you'll be well-positioned to make some goals and decide on the steps you'll take to reach them. Your initial data will also be useful in evaluating your progress later, so you don't have to rely on your own subjective opinion. Because as most of us know too well, we can be quite negatively biased when evaluating ourselves.

I'll help you listen to your body and get good initial data on the food you're eating in the Dynamic Lifestyle Road Map at the end of this book. It's an invaluable learning experience that can be both interesting and fun! If you take me up on this activity, it'll boost your success tremendously as you move forward in this journey. I'll provide the details shortly.

Jon Was Overeating and Under-Energized

My client, we'll call him Jon, was sitting in his office at 7 p.m. one evening, perplexed about his eating and energy. He could tell he was having a blood sugar dip because his brain was a little foggy, and he was feeling tired. He was also a bit agitated after two, incredibly long afternoon meetings.

Jon was supposed to head to the gym that night, but he was feeling too hungry and tired. Plus, he had administrative work to finish. So, he ate the leftover Chinese food he had saved in the breakroom fridge the night before and went back to his computer for several hours.

When finally home, he sat on the couch to decompress with two beers and promised himself he'd get to the gym the next day. But it seemed like every day was ending the same way. He couldn't figure out how he could do things differently so the past would stop repeating itself.

Jon wanted to lose weight, improve his blood pressure, and get his energy back. He loved his job and wanted to work for at least another 10 years, but he needed to get his health on track so he could keep up the pace he'd been maintaining for the last 20. He changed his eating habits on his own but didn't see success. In fact, he thought he was eating less, but he had gained some weight. He was also noticing that since he changed his diet, he was feeling a little more irritable and less patient with people. That's what tipped Jon over the edge to work with me.

During our first week together, he kept track of what he was eating and how he was feeling during the day to include his mood and energy levels. It was this first, simple step that revealed most of Jon's problems. His motivation wasn't the problem; he was sticking to his decisions on dietary change. But he had made some less-than-optimal decisions about that change.

As we reviewed his food journal, Jon shared how he was having breakfast at home before leaving for work in the morning, which helped him skip the large vanilla latte and doughnut that he used to get from a local coffee shop. He liked this change because he felt better in the morning and had more energy until about noon.

When it was time for lunch, he'd have a protein bar and a bottle of protein-fortified, natural fruit and vegetable juice. This was in place of what he used to have, which was usually an Italian sub or fast-food burger. He told me he often felt impatient and easily aggravated around midday. "Hangry" was how he explained it, jokingly. To fix this, he'd have another bar and protein drink. He told me that his new lunch plan took a lot of willpower. He was disheartened because despite the fact he thought he was dieting and eating healthier, he wasn't losing weight or feeling more energy. Instead, he had gained a little weight and was feeling a little digestive discomfort. He was also disappointed that he still couldn't muster the energy to go to the gym after long days at work.

There were multiple reasons why Jon's new plan wasn't working for him and he figured out a few of those reasons while journaling. His biggest surprise came while examining the nutrition labels on his new lunch. After looking closer at the label on the back of the drink, Jon couldn't believe that the small, "natural" juice drink he was drinking had 300 calories. And for a drink that was mostly fruit and vegetables, it had much more sugar than he expected. To add insult to injury, he found that the protein bar he was eating, which was smaller than his palm, had almost 400 calories. Altogether, Jon was eating about 700 calories with just those two items. "After two hours, it didn't even feel like I had eaten anything," he said, with disappointment. "How is that possible?" On the afternoons when John had this snack twice, he was eating almost 1,400 calories.

It's a good time to break from the story and explain the single most important concept you need to know to make your best decisions about food, now and into the future.

Nutrient Density
Nutrient density is a fundamental concept taught in formal nutrition programs, but everyone who eats should understand

this concept. Although there's a scientific calculation for it, you won't have to do any math here. You'll have a stronger sense of what it means and be able to use it to your greatest advantage as you continue reading. For now, here are two definitions you should know:

1. Nutrient-dense foods are high in nutrients and low in calories.

2. Calorie-dense foods are high in calories but low in nutrients.

Put simply, the more nutrient-dense your food is, the more bang for the buck you're going to get from the calories you're eating. The more calorie-dense your food is, the more calories you'll get with little additional benefit. More to come on that, so stick with me.

Back to Jon's Story

Jon felt cheated when he found out his "healthy" substitutes from the health food section of the grocery store didn't live up to his expectations. Sadly, John had fallen for the "health halo effect." It's a term used for foods that are thought by the public to be much healthier than they really are because of marketing hype and misinformation in the media. I'll help you avoid the health halo effect of many foods as we go along.

Jon was particularly alarmed at the number of calories in his snack, especially because they didn't help him feel full or satisfied. I shared with him that for the 700 calories he ate in the protein bar and drink he could have eaten seven medium sweet potatoes! Granted, not many people can or would eat seven sweet potatoes at one sitting. But if he did, he would certainly *feel like* he had eaten!

To be more realistic, for 730 calories, he could eat two whole chicken breasts, four cups of dark-green salad, and a medium baked potato with a full tablespoon of butter. That's a pretty substantial meal. And all that would total about the same calories of Jon's first lunchtime "snack." It would be very filling to say the least. And it would provide him with an abundance of nutrients, as well as fiber and water, without all the extra sugar. Now that's a nutrient-dense meal!

On top of that, Jon needed food that would keep his digestive system happy and not give him stomach cramps throughout the day. We planned how he'd get a nutrient-dense, nutritionally balanced lunch. With the calories he had to spare, he got to eat a smaller, balanced meal (aka snack) later in the day, which gave him the energy he needed to go the gym. He was much, much happier with this plan.

Step 1—Starting Off Strong

During this step you'll simply gather data. Don't change a thing about what you eat; just document it. To the best of your ability, write down what you eat and how much you eat. In addition, take notes on how you feel. Document things like energy, mood, sleep, pain, and productivity. I'll guide you in making observations in the Dynamic Lifestyle Road Map at the back of the book.

This is a crucial step for you for several reasons: first, you'll discover whether change is needed. Instead of hoping that your daily food choices will provide you with the energy you need to be the leader you want to be, you'll take a real look at whether that's actually happening.

Second, you'll discover where change is needed and why. By keeping track of what you eat and how you feel, associations between your food and your energy, mood, brainpower, sleep, and other leadership-critical functions that weren't obvious before will reveal themselves to you. Discovering these details on your own will provide you with a rich and memorable learning experience that you'll use for a lifetime.

Finally, this first step you're taking is one of the biggest secrets to successful and lasting dietary habits change. The biggest reason diets fail is because they change everything about what a person eats, all at once, with a prescription for a complete overhaul. A diet asks you to change your entire food system into something foreign that may not fit into your schedule or accommodate your preferences. It may not even be optimal for your body or digestive system.

We don't get baseline data when we follow a diet, so we don't know which changes made a difference. Once finished with a diet, most people go back to what they used to eat and what they were comfortable with. In doing so, they return to all the old habits that were a problem in the first place.

Unfortunately, this cycle usually ends up with a dieter worse off than when they started: the body usually bounces back to higher weight and with even more food sensitivity than before the diet began. To top it off, it leaves a dieter back at square one, not knowing how to make food work to their advantage in all circumstances of a busy, active, and full life.

This step is your initial data-gathering stage. It's not intended to be a means for you to judge yourself. It's simply information that will be very useful as you move forward. You'll be able to look back at what you used to do and see if the changes you've made since then are for the better. Most likely, all your data will change in a very positive way by the time you finish reading this book and taking the steps I recommend.

The more information you gather in this step, the better equipped you'll be to decide what changes will be best for you and your life based on my future recommendations. Out of all the steps in this book, this will be the most energy you'll spend. Play this full-out because the payoff can be big for you, as it has been for most of my clients and students—read on to see what I mean. Yours can be one of the many success stories!

It's Your Choice

Research has found that when we're embarking on a dietary habit change, keeping detailed notes about the food we're eating provides improved results and longer-lasting change. It also contributes to greater success in weight loss if that's something you're interested in. There are a few ways you can successfully complete this step and get some great initial data on yourself this week. Choose one.

1. Use an app. If you want to get numerical data on calories, nutrients, vitamins, and other specifics, log all your food in an app (most have options on the phone and computer). Additionally, journal regularly about how you feel before and after eating. An app offers a huge return on your investment because you get immediate feedback on the nutrition and calories in the food you're eating. See my notes in The Leading Edge section on how to make the best use of an app if you choose this level.

2. Just write. You can skip the app and write your meals and observations in the Dietary Lifestyle Road Map for a week. You'll have a rich source of information that can reveal a lot to you as you move forward.

3. Take a small bite. If taking notes for a week sounds daunting, commit to journaling for just three days in an app or on paper. Pick days when you eat your most normal meals. You probably have a few go-to meals for breakfast, lunch, and dinner. Try to capture them in your log and observe your physical feelings, emotions, and energy levels after eating and throughout the day. Some information is better than none, and this is a fine place to start.

The Big Payoff

Almost all my clients who have completed this step have discovered something that surprises them. And not all my clients are new to this concept. In fact, at least half of them have journaled foods before, have counted calories in the past, or are already very conscious of what they eat. Why do they get surprised then? Because our bodies, our lives, and our eating patterns change over time.

Novice or not, there are a couple of big payoffs for

journaling your food in the way I'm suggesting. First, the simple act of writing down what you eat and how you feel will help you stop and think, if only for a moment, about whether or not your food is serving you. It'll help you to choose foods consciously rather than unconsciously.

Second, you'll be sharpening your skills of listening to your body's signals during this experience. The only way to know whether your food choices are meeting your needs, both physically and mentally, is by paying attention to what you're eating and how you're responding. If you've never done so, this is a good, solid place to start. If you're already in tune with your body, it will still benefit you to hone in a little more on this.

Listening to your body is a skill that brings unique leadership benefits as well. Our body not only has reactions to food but also reactions to experiences, people, events, and circumstances. This is part of our intuition or "gut reaction." Our bodies can pick up on things that may not show up in hard data. Being connected to intuition is a decision-making skill of great leaders.

After a meal is a good time to take a quiet moment, breathe, and sense how your body feels. Even better—take a short walk outside, listen to the birds, look at the sky, and pay attention to how you feel. Aside from your reactions to food, you may become aware of physical reactions to other things on your mind. You may be surprised at what your body signals can reveal to you regarding upcoming leadership decisions and more. Paying attention to physical reactions to food is a good way to begin paying more attention to your "gut" feelings. From there, you can develop your skills of listening to the physical signs and signals that contribute to your intuition on a larger scale.

It's not necessary for you to journal and log all your food and responses much longer than a week. Although, some of my students find the exercise so helpful that they continue do it for a couple of months. For now, commit to this for one week—

seven days.

Surprises Await You

One of my clients, I'll call her Brenda, was a cancer survivor and held a high-level decision-making position in the U.S. federal government. To assist her battle with cancer, she adopted an extremely clean eating plan and kept it ever since. Unlike Jon, she was a competitive athlete. But she carried extra weight around her middle that she couldn't lose. She had pretty much decided that as a woman over 40, her body was just going to be that way from now on.

After completing this initial step with me, she found that even though her meals were mostly clean and healthy, she had fallen for the health halo effect with some foods, like Jon. I'll share more about her specific food selections later. At this time, I'll tell you that Brenda was eating too many calories from her "healthy" choices. Even though she was very active, it was a major reason she had been holding on to unwanted weight for years. By the end of our work together, she had replaced these calorie-dense foods with nutrient-dense foods, and to her surprise, her extra weight disappeared.

Weight loss isn't everyone's goal, so swapping high-calorie foods for lower-calorie foods may not be what you need. Some of my clients realize they're eating when they're not hungry and find better ways to destress and take their mind off work. Others find that the foods unsettling their stomach are not the foods they initially thought were to blame. Others discover that their eating schedule doesn't support their energy needs. The list of what my students discover from this step goes on and on. I'm excited for you to get this experience and the deeper knowledge it reveals about how food affects your body, your mind, and your leadership abilities.

Maximize Your Opportunity for Success

Here are a few tricks that'll help you to easily master this important, first step.

1. Curiosity is a big motivator. Pique your curiosity before you start; think of what you'd most like to discover. Do you wonder whether something you're eating is causing you to be tired or bloated or have brain fog? Are you interested in what foods bring you the most stamina? Are you curious about what foods might help you calm down at night after a long day? You'll begin answering your questions in this step with data, instead of guessing.

2. Free up your brain space. Write down what you eat and how you're feeling as close to mealtime as possible, so you don't have to use valuable brain energy to remember all the food you ate for the entire day. If you leave your documentation until the end of the day, it can feel like a chore. If you leave it for more than a day, you might not do it. However you decide to complete this step, write your notes as soon as possible and throughout the day if you can.

3. Take a look at "If You Don't Have Measuring Tools" in The Leading Edge section for ways to estimate amounts of food so you can get familiar with how much food you're eating. This will be of great use while you continue learning about your food choices.

4. Bring your knowledge into life. If you feel comfortable, share with someone about what you're discovering through your food journaling project. Ask if you can be accountable to them for completing your goals. Someone you eat with is an ideal candidate.

5. Take action as soon as possible. Begin writing what you ate and how you felt today in your personal, Dynamic Lifestyle Road Map.

THE LEADING EDGE OF SUCCESS

That was the end of the big picture information. The Leading Edge section, in the second half of each chapter, will provide extra details that'll give you an edge when it comes to succeeding in each step. Since I've worked with hundreds of people on taking these steps, topics here will address the most common questions I've gotten regarding the information we're covering. I'll also dive deeper into certain subjects that may warrant a little more attention. You can read it all or choose the topics that interest you most.

To expand your knowledge even further, take a look at the References and the "Additional Good Reads" section at the back of the book. You can get even more resources and connect with me further about food and leadership at EatToLead.com.

How to Use an App for the Greatest Return on Your Investment

If you decide to use one of the free apps available online, you can get quality data on your food like calories, protein, carbs, and fat, as well as the balance of your vitamins and minerals that you won't get when using a paper record. Here's how to use an app to get the most out of the small amount of time you invest in tracking:

1. An app is always with you on your phone. Take advantage of that and use your phone to log your food immediately before or after you eat it.

2. Have the app remember your foods, meals, and recipes. Most apps will remember your most recent input so you can easily select the same items the next time. You can also save and name the meals you eat regularly (like *breakfast egg sandwich, chicken tortilla lunch*, etc.). It will take more effort in the first few days, but if you eat the same meals frequently, it'll make things significantly faster and easier moving forward.

3. If you eat most of your meals out, most apps today have big databases of nutrition information about restaurant food and brand-name foods. Just search and select it in the finder. There's usually an option to take a picture of the bar code or scan the QR code on packaged foods to quickly get the most

accurate information.

4. If you can't find what you're eating, improvise. Find food that's similar and enter it. But try to be as close as possible to get the most accurate information.

5. After you've finished the logging exercises in this book, you can use your app more sporadically. You can plan meals in advance or spot-check nutrient information in foods you want to know more about. This will help you make sure any new food you're planning to eat meets your standards and avoid adding big mistakes to your regular menu.

Reverse Measure: The Best Way to Know What You're Eating

While taking this step, I suggest reverse measuring your food. What I mean is, rather than measuring your food to portion it out, use measuring utensils to serve yourself what you normally eat.

Using measuring tools like measuring cups and spoons and a food scale for a short amount of time will help you get to know what food portions look like on your plate. Moving forward, you'll be able to identify portions of food wherever you are—at home, eating out, while traveling, even in a different country. It'll help you avoid the negative effects of eating too much food (which is more than just weight gain, as you'll soon see), and avoid eating too much of the wrong food. But for now, just eat normally and measure it.

Even though I've been coaching people on this for a long time, I get measuring tools out in my own kitchen on a regular basis. Sometimes I'm evaluating a new meal I'm making. Sometimes I want to see how much of a particular food fits on a certain plate, in a bowl, or glass I have at home so in the future, I can estimate by sight how much to serve myself and others.

If You Don't Have Measuring Tools

When you don't have measuring utensils on hand, here are some easy references for estimating food portions:

One cup = the size of a baseball or your closed fist

One tablespoon = a poker chip or your entire thumb

Three ounces = the size of a deck of cards or the palm of your hand

One ounce = the size of a golf ball, two dice, or your entire thumb.

Do Calories Count?

Maybe you've been hearing from popular media or certain weight loss gurus that calories don't really matter in the whole scheme of things. But that's not true.

Calories are the measurement of fuel that we get from food that our body then burns or puts into storage. Calories are the unit of measurement that all nutrition professionals and nutrition scientists use. Saying "calories don't count" is like saying "inches don't count" or "quarters don't count." These are all units of measurement, and they count when they're used to measure human fuel, distance, and money, respectively.

If we overeat calories, we gain weight. This premise hasn't been disproven, even though popular books, the news, and social media might have you believing that it has. Keep in mind, though, that calories are always an estimation. What I mean is, do you always eat a perfectly measured medium apple? Do you always burn exactly 1,200 calories—or whatever your resting metabolic rate is—on the days you don't exercise? (The answer to both of those is no.) Even so, these measurements help us compare and contrast the fuel we get from food and how much energy we burn.

There are 3,500 calories in a pound of fat. But it takes everyone a different amount of time to accumulate or burn that number because we all have different bodies, digestive systems, and lifestyles. Yet eating just 500 calories over and above what you need for five days per week, adds up to 130,000 calories in a year. And that has the potential to turn into 37 pounds of fat on your body in a year. The sad part is, like Jon, you can eat thousands of extra calories and not feel energy or satisfaction from your food.

The topic of calories is only one of the many food concepts we discuss in this book, and we'll move on to additional topics in the next chapters. It's necessary, however, to know a little about calories because they play a role in making good decisions on food. Most importantly, your knowledge will help you determine whether the food you're eating is nutrient-dense or calorie-dense.

If you don't use an app and you simply take notes, you may not get calorie or nutrient estimations for all your food, but you can still investigate labels and check out nutrition data where it's available. Whatever knowledge you gain in this first step and any notes you take will help you make significantly better decisions about food long into the future.

What Foods Give You Energy?

As a leader, it's important to know where your energy comes from so you can get it and maintain it when you need it. Before I went back to school for nutrition, I thought energy from food was supposed to feel like caffeine. At least that's what I was looking for! But I never got that feeling from food, no matter how much I ate. As it turns out, that's not what food energy feels like.

Energy from food is subtler than caffeine. During and after a meal, if you pay attention, you can feel an uptick in energy. It's not going to smack you in the back of the head like coffee. It won't ramp you up like tea or provide the jump-start you feel from yerba mate or any other stimulant. But, for some time after you eat the right foods, if you're listening to your body, you'll feel a steady stream of energy to think clearer, move faster, continue being productive, and make good decisions.

The right food energy at the right times will not only help your brain work better and help you perform at higher levels during the day, it will also help you get better results from your workouts and sleep better at night.

Popular media frequently suggests that one, magic food can give us all the energy we need, cure anything that ails us, and make us young again to boot. But there's no cure-all food or supplement, and our best energy doesn't come from a single food. Rather, all foods complement each other to offer the vitality and vibrancy that you're looking for. In addition, the amount of energy we get from our food depends on many things: how much we eat, when we eat, where we get the food from, and the combinations of food we eat. All of which you'll be discovering more about as you progress through this book.

Another thing to keep in mind is that energy is defined in science as "the ability to do work." Energy for the human body and brain is provided in the form of calories. If we were to compare the human body to a car, we could say that just like a car uses gas that's measured in gallons, humans use food that's measured in calories. Although there are about eight major nutrient categories (protein, carbs, fat, vitamins, minerals, antioxidants, phytochemicals, and water), we only use three of these nutrients for fuel. They're called macronutrients because they're the nutrients that provide us with the majority of our calories, and they're the nutrients we need to eat most to survive and function. They are:

- Protein

- Carbohydrates

- Fat

Other nutrients don't give us fuel or energy. They're more like "building blocks for the body." Going back to the car example: the car doesn't use things like metal, leather, rubber, glass, windshield washer fluid, or the engine itself for fuel. But nicer leather and upholstery will make the car look better, and a better engine will make it more powerful. Likewise, humans use nutrients other than protein, carbohydrates, and fat for purposes other than fuel, and they affect our performance and how we look and feel. For that reason, an antioxidant drink or a vitamin won't give you energy, but it can have other benefits.

Here's some additional information to keep in mind as you observe and document your energy and begin making decisions about how to get more of it from food. I'll expand on all of this in future chapters:

- Overeating any food can make you sleepy. At the very least, you'll be uncomfortable in your gut and bloated until you've digested. Many have misidentified this simple, natural response as an allergic reaction to food when all it takes is smaller serving sizes.

- How a food has been prepared will affect your energy. For example, if your food is covered with heavy, creamy, or buttery sauce, soaked or cooked in oil or fat, or any other high-calorie additive, it will take longer to digest. That means it can stay in your digestive system longer, diverting energy from your brain and elsewhere, and make you feel tired and sluggish for a while.

- Foods high in sugar, especially when eaten alone, will give you an initial burst of energy and can leave you ravenously hungry shortly afterward.

- If you don't eat enough, you can find yourself tired. But during starvation or semistarvation, you can feel unusually energized due to the increase of stress hormones in your body. High-stress hormones for long periods are detrimental to our body and brain. So, we want to be sure we're getting enough fuel regularly.

Your energy is also influenced by factors other than food:

- Your mindset, as well as your attitude and emotions, will

affect your energy levels because your thoughts create the chemicals (like adrenaline, serotonin, and dopamine) that flow through your blood and circle back to your brain.

• Not getting enough sleep or being under high levels of stress for long periods will dampen any energy you might otherwise get from your food.

• Different seasons can cause us to feel differently about foods. For example, you may like the feeling a heavier meal brings in the winter but dislike that feeling in the summer. Pay attention to outside factors that may be influencing your like or dislike for the way a food makes you feel.

To get a valid picture of the energy your food provides, it's helpful to be aware of, and document as much as you can, what else in your life is going on that can be affecting your energy. Every bit of this data will help you understand more fully how food affects your leadership capacity.

Be Exceptional

Gathering data is important for making decisions. Exceptional leaders gather data as well as listen to those who'll be impacted by a decision to make the best decisions possible. They also tune in to their intuition. Now is the time to listen to yourself and tune in to your "gut" so you can make the best decisions possible when it comes to changing your eating habits. Head over to the Dynamic Lifestyle Road Map where I'll guide you in collecting your initial data. In the next step, I'll help you set goals based on your data, and I'll lead you in making the single most important change to your diet that will have the biggest, positive impact on your physical and mental performance, your health, and your life.

| CHAPTER 2 |
GOALS AND THE MOST IMPORTANT THING

I acknowledge you for working on changing your body and life for the better and for the long run. Your investment in this activity will drive exponential gains in your health and the future of your leadership in ways you may not even begin to imagine at this time. Be on the watch for pleasant surprises! There's nothing like the motivation you'll get when you start to see and feel the benefits, large and small, that come from taking consistent steps toward your goals of eating better food.

Goal Setting and Motivation

Leaders don't just have big goals; they reach big goals and help others reach them too. As you've likely discovered, setting goals and reaching them are not one and the same. We need to have good decision-making skills for setting goals, but one of the most important factors in reaching a goal is that everyone involved is motivated.

Michael Csikszentmihalyi, author of *Flow: The Psychology of Optimal Experience*, talks about the benefits of setting "stretch goals." Stretch goals are goals that match and slightly stretch your current skill level. According to Csikszentmihalyi, when you set this kind of goal, you're more likely to reach it. Even more importantly, you're much more likely to enjoy the work you're doing while pursuing it.

Leaders who use stretch goals set people up for success and keep motivation high. When we're enjoying the process, we don't mind working toward a goal. Not to mention, achieving a goal is motivation in itself; success breeds success. Ultimately, stretch goals taken step by step, one after the other, add up to bigger accomplishments and greater satisfaction from achieving them.

When unexpected challenges and roadblocks come up on the road to reaching goals, people look to leaders for help. Leaders think outside the box to reach goals. They innovate and use creative thinking to get over, around, and through obstacles. Exceptional leaders go a step further—they provide people with tools and knowledge so they can eventually overcome obstacles on their own.

I'm going to help you set some stretch goals for eating the right food. In each of these next steps, I'll help you select a level of change that meets you where you are and slightly stretches your skills to keep your new experiences with food enjoyable. You'll gain some tools and knowledge that will help you fit these steps into your busy, leadership life. And I'll help you get used to thinking outside the box to get over, around, or through obstacles and keep moving forward so you can receive all the benefits food has to offer!

What and Why

In this particular step, I'll help you make the single most important change to your diet that will have the biggest, positive impact on your physical and mental performance, your health, and your life. When you get this part down, say goodbye to fad diets, crazy food gimmicks, or quick fixes because you won't need any of them. And when you succeed at this, which you will, you'll be even more motivated to keep going.

Judi's Struggle

It was 10 p.m. and Judi was just sitting down in her home office to start a couple more hours of work. She was an entrepreneur and mom of two young children. Since she had her first child, she had been suffering from inexplicable pains throughout her body and a constant barrage of illnesses. She was also having trouble sleeping despite the fact that her children had been sleeping through the night for some time. She went to work exhausted every day. On the days she had physical pain, she'd go to work and push through anyway. But she found it difficult to think. The fatigue and frequent illnesses were decreasing her productivity and creativity, and she had to make up for it by putting in more hours of work late into the night after her children went to bed.

It was a catch-22 she couldn't get out of. She needed her job because her family needed the income. She was often irritable and impatient because of how she felt, but she worked hard to hide it to avoid negatively affecting her relationships at home and at work. She was tired and needed sleep to do the creative thinking that was required of her, but she couldn't sleep more because she needed to make up for lost productivity by working into the night.

She had been to many health professionals and hadn't found an explanation, let alone a cure for her issues. She had cut out dairy and bread, which she felt helped a little. She was also taking several high-priced supplements. But she was still struggling. She had asked me if there was anything she could possibly do through nutrition to help her feel better. My first piece of advice to her was to do exactly what you'll start doing in this step. She wanted to feel better so badly that, true to her detail-oriented, precision-oriented leadership style, she followed my advice to the letter.

Afterward, her body changed quickly. Her random pains and illness went away almost completely. She stopped having indigestion and headaches. Because she felt better, she started sleeping better. And all of this added up to more patience with the people she worked with, and her children, and more creativity and mental energy for her work. To top it off, she lost about 12 pounds without even trying. It sounds too good to be true, doesn't it? Even I was surprised at her profound results! Everyone's results vary, but that's what happened to her.

Plant Foods are the Most Important Thing

There are reams of research showing that eating at least five servings per day of fruits and vegetables helps to prevent innumerable illnesses and diseases, including the top killers in the U.S.: cancer, heart disease, stroke, Alzheimer's, and type 2 diabetes. It will bolster your immune system, reduce inflammation, protect your brain, and create a body and mind that is more youthful and resilient. The American Heart Association, CDC, WHO, American Diabetes Association, American Dietetic Association, USDA, and agencies around the world acknowledge this as one of the best things you can do for your health and longevity. In fact, five servings per day are healthy, but more is even better. And I'll tell you from experience, few people get the minimum.

Do you? If you look back at your log from last week, you can quickly see if you are. The good news is, I'll help you to get more than the minimum recommendation every day, with ease.

The benefits that come from these plant foods are in large part because they're abundant in phytochemicals, antioxidants, vitamins, minerals, and fiber. These are the nutrients that provide the antiaging, anti-inflammatory, immune-boosting, disease-resisting, cancer-fighting properties. These are the magic ingredients that keep your skin looking fresh and youthful, keep your eyes bright and working well, and protect your brain from degradation. They play a key role in keeping your DNA young and can even reverse its aging. They're an important part of the formula for meals I'm revealing to you here that gives you the even-keeled energy and mental focus that you need to be a high-performing leader.

Vegetables are the most nutrient-dense foods by far. They have high levels of nutrition and are extremely low in calories. It's why diet conglomerates like Weight Watchers lists fresh vegetables as a "free food" and pretty much every diet around today includes vegetables in abundance. They're packed with fiber and water and help you feel satisfied without feeling full or tired. You can eat them with abandon if you eat them the right way.

More good news is you never need to do any of the popular "cleanse" diets if you're eating enough vegetables. The first step of cleansing happens in the intestines with fiber from foods like vegetables (and others to be revealed). As the mostly undigestible fiber from vegetables flows through both your large and small intestine, it cleans them. Fiber also helps beneficial bacteria grow and form a healthy microbiome in your intestines, which keeps unhealthy elements from your food out of your blood supply. After that, your liver ensures that your blood is clean and free of toxins. If your liver wasn't doing its job right, you'd know it—you'd need to be hospitalized. That being said, eating vegetables in the way I'm suggesting here and drinking plenty of water will ensure you stay clean from the inside out.

After hearing all this information, it'd be easy to say that vegetables are magic if you didn't know any better. They're certainly the magical ingredient to almost every diet, and today I'm going to help you start getting more of that magic into your life without dieting.

My Story

Like many of my clients, I used to dislike most vegetables. And like many, my dislike started in childhood. Most vegetables I experienced were from a can, sometimes they had freezer burn, and they were usually overcooked. It didn't matter if I was eating at home or a restaurant; I didn't encounter many delicious vegetables. Vegetables from my grandmothers' gardens were the one exception; I surprisingly enjoyed them washed, straight out of the ground. I didn't know the reason I disliked most vegetables was that they weren't prepared in the way vegetables taste best.

The only other vegetables I enjoyed were drowning in

butter or cream or lost under a mound of cheese. When I learned more about cooking food, I learned that this is how you mask mediocre flavor. But we don't need to do this if we know how to choose and prepare vegetables with their exciting tastes intact!

After studying the chemistry of food and cooking, I discovered that less cooking is better for most vegetables. Contrary to many diet fads and myths, research shows cooking doesn't "kill" all the vitamins and render your vegetables worthless. *Overcooking* will reduce the potency of some vitamins. More damage is done with a combination of higher heat and longer cooking times; vitamin C and folate are the most vulnerable. But you will continue to get benefits from vitamins in cooked food. In fact, for denser vegetables like potatoes and parsnips, brussels sprouts and beets, cooking will enhance your ability to digest them. It can also increase your absorption of certain vitamins and antioxidants, like the lycopene in tomatoes or vitamin A in carrots. As a general rule though, minimal cooking preserves taste and texture. And that's the key to the most enjoyable vegetable experience.

When I started experimenting with eating vegetables fresh and lightly cooked, I discovered the unique and natural flavors of this plant food. There can be a rainbow of tastes in your mouth when you eat vegetables for their maximum flavor. And that's what I'll help you discover for yourself this week.

Step 2—The Most Important Thing

Let's move on to the very foundation of what makes most diets succeed and what will bring you the biggest benefit in the shortest amount of time. Eating the right amounts of healthy, nutrient-dense vegetables will help you turn lunches and dinners into delicious meals that satisfy your hunger and can reduce your cravings for sugar, fat, and junk foods to boot. It will help balance your energy, help you have longer run-times in between meals, and keep serious illness at bay. Vegetables are a nutritional "edge" that every vibrant, energetic leader needs. Here's how you'll do it:

1. Make vegetables half of every lunch and dinner. This is how you'll get at least, and sometimes more than, three servings of vegetables every day. That being said, lunches and dinners come in all different sizes, and the official serving sizes of different vegetables are not all the same. So, I've created a generalization that's dependable and works:

• At lunch, construct your meal with at least one serving of vegetables.

• At dinner, construct your meal with at least *two* servings of vegetables and aim for at least two different kinds.

• One serving of vegetables, for your purposes, is (a) one cup chopped, or (b) one large vegetable. For example, one serving is a cup of chopped cucumbers or a large carrot.

• From now on, assume that a cup serving size is equal to the size of your entire closed fist. It's a good approximation. If your fist is slightly bigger than a cup, that is perfectly fine; your serving size will better fit your body size.

Here's how to visualize the structure of these two meals:

2. Eat vegetables in their purest, most natural, and whole form. That means eat them in the way that most resembles how they came from the ground. Eat them raw, steamed, grilled, roasted, or stir-fried in the smallest bit of oil. You can also eat them briefly microwaved or blanched (dropped into boiling water for one to five minutes max). Use as little sauce, butter, cheese, or other additions as possible. We'll call these *clean* vegetables because they're not "dirtied up" by other, less healthy ingredients. While increasing the flavor and the nutrient value, you'll be decreasing the calories, salt, saturated fat, chemicals, preservatives, and other additives—the culprits that can cause energy slumps, fatigue, brain fog, and wreak havoc on your health.

If you feel you need sauce, butter, or cheese, try adding a little less than usual. Subtle tastes can be even more enjoyable than those that overpower. See The Leading Edge for more suggestions in "Creative Vegetable Toppings."

3. Diversify. Each vegetable has its unique combination of vitamins, phytochemicals, and antioxidants. They all have unique and vital roles to play in the optimal functioning of your mind and body. A fun way to look at this is to remember that the predominant vitamins and minerals in a plant show up as specific colors. Eat as many colors throughout the day as possible. The more colors you eat, the wider the range of vitamins, minerals, and phytochemicals you'll get without using a diet app or food database to figure it out. You can discover more about the colors that are related to the nutrients in your vegetables with a quick online search. Start with three words—color, nutrients, and food—and go from there.

One color worth singling out is dark green. There's very exciting emerging research about dark green leafy vegetables; where we used to think that carrots were the key to eye health and good night vision, dark green leafies have taken the lead. Now we're finding they also help maintain your brain health and can improve your executive functioning. Incorporate dark green leafy vegetables into meals as often as possible. For more details, see "Dark Greens Are the New Orange" in The Leading Edge section.

4. Observe and document. Now that you're making changes to your food choices, it'll be helpful to keep notes to see whether they're working. You're creating your personal system for success, and I'll lead you through it in a simple way in your Dynamic Lifestyle Road Map.

5. Bring your learning to life. Eat your vegetables with people you enjoy spending time with and converse a little about the changes you're making and why.

It's Your Choice

If you don't like vegetables, it's okay. I'll help you enjoy these plant foods on your terms. Here are some ways you can accomplish this step this week. Make a stretch goal from this list and get started having fun exploring healthy food in a new way!

1. Eat better while eating out. If you eat out most of the time, order more vegetables with your meals. Entrées at most restaurants come with few vegetables save for a garnish on the plate. When that's the case, order a side dish of vegetables. Here are more things to keep in mind when at a restaurant:

- Look for fresh, grilled, blanched, steamed, baked, or roasted vegetables. Stir-fried in a light sauce works too.

- Ask how they're cooked. Make sure the restaurant doesn't completely ruin your plan to eat healthy by cooking your vegetables with tons of butter, oil, or cheese. What I mean is that deep-fried green beans would be the exact opposite of what we're trying to accomplish here.

- Ask for salad dressings and sauces on the side, so you have control of any additional ingredients.

- If you order vegetables that come with cheese, oil, butter,

47

or other toppings, ask the chef to "go light" on them.

2. Replace junk food with vegetables. Swap vegetables for processed food like cookies, doughnuts, and coffee cake. Eat them with takeout meals and sandwiches instead of chips. This will increase your meal satisfaction and reduce your risk of having a sugar crash that can undermine your energy for the rest of the day.

If you're still hungry after a meal, your body is telling you you're not finished getting all the nutrients you need. Make another, smaller plate of the same meal, in the same manner— with half vegetables. Or, eat another serving of vegetables and see where that takes you. Don't go for chips or dessert when your body is asking for more nutrients.

I've never asked any client to completely avoid chips, dessert, or anything else that they love. We should be able to enjoy foods that give us pleasure. Yet, these are treats, meant to be eaten in small quantities. We eat these only after we've eaten what our body and mind need and truly craves for optimal performance, which is real food.

3. Be proactive. At the beginning of the week, stock up on vegetables that are easy to eat. Make time to prepare them for easy access during the week. Keep some at home and take some to work to improve your meals and snacks there. On the days you come home tired and hungry with less willpower and motivation, you can add your ready-to-eat vegetables to any meal: add them to a stir-fry, steam or bake them, or eat them raw.

4. Get picky. If you're ready to take the taste and nutrient level of your vegetables up a notch, get more discriminating about quality. The freshest vegetables are in the produce section of your grocery store, not in the packaged or processed aisles. Those that are bright in color and firm to the touch will be at the peak of flavor. You'll enjoy eating the freshest vegetables much more, and they'll last longer in your refrigerator. For more details, check out "Why Local, in Season,

Tastes Best" in The Leading Edge section of the chapter.

Maximize Your Opportunity for Success

Since I've worked with so many people on this step, I'm familiar with the most common questions and misconceptions. I'll address a few here and save you from making common mistakes.

Does vegetable sauce (like tomato sauce) count as a vegetable?

Tomato sauce offers vitamins, like vitamin C, and phytochemicals, including cancer-fighting lycopene. When purchasing it in a jar or can, look for the brand lowest in added sugar and salt. Although it can provide some healthy nutrients, it's not the whole-form vegetable that I want you to focus on. Eat it, but don't count it as a serving of vegetables.

Does vegetable juice count as a vegetable?

Drinking fresh vegetable juice can be a great way to get more vitamins into your day, but don't count it as one of your three servings. The key is to *eat* your vegetables. I'll share more about why you want to eat instead of drink your food in the next chapter.

Do lettuce and tomato on a sandwich count as a serving?

Sandwich trimmings are a great way to add vegetables. But don't consider them a serving unless you're sure they add up to a cup or more of vegetables. Add fresh vegetables or a side salad to your plate to reach your goal. More is always better, so load up on those sandwich veggies as much as possible anyway.

What about hummus and guacamole?

These have great nutrition in small doses. Hummus is made from garbanzo beans, and guacamole is made with avocado—two beneficial foods that I talk about in future chapters. But they're calorie concentrated. Different from the vegetables we're focusing on here, they're best described as healthier versions of calorie-dense toppings and dips. Have some, because they offer healthy fats, and eat them along with other, water-filled, fiber-dense vegetables.

Can I have a giant salad for lunch and be done with vegetables for the day?

I don't recommend it. Eating vegetables with most meals will distribute your nutrients and help manage your energy levels. You'll understand this more fully as you continue reading. But as an overview, I'll share that eating vegetables in the afternoon will help you feel light and unburdened from your meal, so you can keep speeding through your day. And eating vegetables at dinner will help you be more satisfied with fewer calories and feel less heavy before bed. I've got more tips on salad in The Leading Edge section.

You Can Succeed at This

After this exercise, many of my students start enjoying vegetables more. I'll never forget when one of my students was overjoyed to report he had a vegetarian meal and didn't miss meat at all. He was someone who, in the past, thought he needed meat in every meal to feel satisfied. It was a big deal for him, and I was excited *for* him! I'm not trying to turn you into a vegetarian, but as you now know, vegetables are very beneficial, and most of us need to be eating many more of them. My client didn't become a vegetarian, but he ended up eating meat-free meals once in a while. A vegetarian meal now and then would certainly be a fine experiment for you to try, too.

Another one of my students told me that her husband of 35 years got so excited about experimenting with new food that he started doing the grocery shopping for the first time ever. She was both amazed and pleasantly surprised that her husband was even open to this completely new activity. My hope is that you experience this kind of enjoyment and excitement for trying new activities around healthy foods and involve your friends and loved ones too. Having good food experiences with people you enjoy spending time with is both motivating and rewarding.

THE LEADING EDGE OF SUCCESS

These extra details will give you an edge when it comes to succeeding in each step. You can read it all or choose the topics that interest you most.

Beware of the After-Work Danger Zone

The *after-work danger zone* is what I call the time before dinner, right after you come home from work, exhausted and hungry. This is when many people grab a snack of crackers, nuts, cheese, or chips, and a serving or two of alcohol. Most of the time it's mindless eating, and most don't even remember what they ate during that time.

Recall my story from the last chapter—700 calories can be eaten in the blink of an eye without filling you up or satisfying you like a real meal. During this dangerous time, you can easily ingest all your calories for the evening before you've had dinner, without even noticing.

One of the best ways to avoid the after-work danger zone is by eating fresh vegetables before dinner. I bring baby carrots to the counter, and my husband and I dig into them while preparing our meal or on the rare occasion when we're waiting for restaurant delivery. I eat as many baby carrots as I want without overeating my calories for the evening or filling up too much before dinner. At the same time, I get extra vitamins A and C, potassium, and more cancer-fighting, immune-boosting, inflammation-reducing phytochemicals packed with copious amounts of water and fiber. It doesn't need to be carrots; any vegetable will do. When prepping food by myself,

I'll rinse and eat a whole English cucumber, bite into a big bell pepper, or enjoy a bowl of cherry tomatoes. By the time dinner is ready, I've eaten at least a serving of vegetables.

On that note, minimally prepared, fresh vegetables are an excellent change of pace and perfectly acceptable at the dinner table. In the summer, I'll throw carrots in one bowl, farmer's market cherry tomatoes in another, and place them at the center of the table. Even my dinner guests happily eat them as part of the meal. As long as the vegetables taste good, no one feels like they're missing anything. Don't think twice about being unconventional when it comes to eating vegetables. Think outside the box.

Dark Greens Are the New Orange

Carrots are still associated with healthy eyes, but dark green leafy vegetables are coming to the forefront of the conversation regarding prevention and protection. The antioxidants abundant in these vegetables—lutein and zeaxanthin—have been found to accumulate in the eyes, and significantly reduce the risk of age-related macular degeneration and protect night vision.

Exciting, emerging research shows that these phyto-chemicals can also accumulate in our brain, higher levels of which are associated with better brain performance in executive functioning, language, learning, and memory. They can also reduce our risk of dementia. Eat more of these greens now to support your brain in leadership functions and maintain its optimal functioning long into the future.

The dark greens with the most lutein and zeaxanthin are kale and spinach. Dr. Martha Morris, author of *Diet for the Mind*, recommends we eat a cup of these every day. I say, make it a goal to eat these powerful dark greens at least four times per week for their brain-boosting benefits.

Salad—Make It Good or Don't Make It at All

I'm not a big salad person. Years ago, I'd have eaten a salad for lunch or dinner to keep my weight down, just like everyone else. I didn't understand why, after having a large salad, I'd get so hungry an hour or so afterward. After a few years into my study of nutrition, I figured out the following:

1. Meal-type salads are usually loaded with calorie-dense items like dressings, cheese, deep-fried noodles, chips, and croutons. Some salads can cost you a thousand calories or more. Even with all those calories, most are still devoid of the good nutrients and satisfaction that you can get—and need to get—from a real meal. One of my clients and I figured out that the salads he had been eating for lunch were at least 2,000 calories! Like Jon, he was trying to be healthy.

2. Many restaurants use iceberg lettuce as a base. It has the least nutrients out of all the greens used for salad.

3. Salads are not usually made with the specific meal proportions I'm giving you here. Therefore, they're missing critical ingredients that contribute to keeping you satisfied and energized for hours.

Your body doesn't get satisfied from the number of calories you eat. Instead, you feel satisfied from the feeling you have in your gut that tells you you've eaten, and the hormones your body releases in response to a balanced meal. So, even if you eat a 1,000-calorie salad, you can still feel hungry shortly afterward because you won't have the filled and satisfied feeling you normally get after eating a meal. This leads to being "hangry" shortly afterward, as Jon puts it, and with less energy for your brain to perform optimally for the rest of the day.

Today you'll find more salads made with spinach, kale, arugula, mixed greens, or spring mix as a base, which are much more nutrient-dense. Along with the benefits of lutein and zeaxanthin, spinach and kale are heavier than lettuce and more filling. But I still don't recommend having salad as a stand-alone meal. The best way to eat any salad is along with protein and carbohydrates in the correct proportions. A salad can be one of your vegetable servings if it's at least a cup of nutrient-dense vegetables. And make sure it isn't overloaded with unnecessary calories from dressings, cheeses, and deep-fried items.

Why Local, in Season, Tastes Best

Local produce is usually the freshest and best tasting because it hasn't ripened on a truck. Truck-ripened vegetables are often picked early and then ripened (sometimes artificially) as they travel to their destination. Because these plants spend less time in the ground absorbing beneficial nutrients, they also taste less than optimal.

If you can't find good-tasting, fresh vegetables at your grocery store, see if there's a farmer's market near you where food comes directly from the farmer. Fresher vegetables sometimes cost a little more, but they ultimately have greater value: not only do they taste better, but they last longer in the fridge. You'll save money and time by not throwing half of them out once they've gone bad by the end of the week.

Secrets of Five-Star Restaurants

When I was working 12- to 14-hour days including weekends, whenever I cooked for myself, I was tired, in a rush, and hungry. I didn't find it relaxing and definitely didn't find it enjoyable. Of course, not much is enjoyable when you're tired and hungry.

I also didn't know how to put food together in a way that tasted optimal. Sometimes my home-prepared meals looked and tasted good. Sometimes they looked bad but tasted good; sometimes they looked and tasted bad.

When I went out to eat, it was always a struggle to get food that was healthy. Even if a meal sounds healthy on the menu, in reality, it can turn out to be much less healthy. Healthy food that also tastes good is the hardest to find at restaurants.

Cooking still isn't something I'm drawn to. I like to get things done fast and efficiently. Because of that, I make meals unconventionally and with shortcuts. The difference between now and then is that now I make food that's healthy and fast, fuels my brain and body for optimal performance, and also tastes good!

You may be so tired after long hours at work that you don't have the energy or patience to make a meal. For that reason, you may eat out or order in most of the time. Or maybe you think that if you do make a meal, it needs to be a recipe with lots of steps, lots of planning, and many ingredients. Let me absolve you of that now. You don't need to make a fancy meal every time you cook unless you enjoy it. But for most people, especially during the week, it's too much work.

In each Leading Edge section, you'll find my "Secrets of Five-Star Restaurants." I'll share shortcuts to making—and eating—simple, fast, healthy meals that look and taste like they've come from an exceptional restaurant and also provide the satisfaction you crave and the energy you need to be a high-performing leader. This will make healthy eating much more enjoyable for you.

It's possible that once you're done with your journey through the pages of this book, you'll be making meals for yourself that you think are better tasting than some five-star restaurants. And you'll feel better afterward to boot. In fact, you just might become so confident that your healthy food is also delicious that you'll even serve it to friends. That's what eventually happened to me. Now, I make meals confidently for groups. My guests are usually surprised and always grateful to find out that the food they're eating and enjoying isn't going to make them feel physically terrible or psychologically guilty the next day.

Your first five-star restaurant secret is this: simple meals can taste amazing! No doubt you've gone to a restaurant and had a simple yet elegant meal that looked beautiful on the plate and was also very delicious. It's these simple, elegant meals that we usually pay a much higher price for and get unbelievable satisfaction from eating. Ask any five-star chef and they'll tell you that high-quality, fresh ingredients are the single most important factor in preparing meals with excellent taste. Start there, and you don't need to worry about much else. This food doesn't need to be masked with heavy sauces, cheeses, or other flavor enhancements—you can taste the delicious flavor of a high-quality ingredient on its own. If you've read up to this point, you know how to choose vegetables for maximum flavor and enjoyment. Start with that this week: choose fresh vegetables to go with your meals and keep it simple.

Creative Vegetable Toppings
You may be surprised by how few additions you need to enjoy vegetables when they're fresh. I won't go into why you'd want to eat less cheese or oil in this chapter, because I talk about it in detail in chapter 6.

When it comes to cheese, try using a stronger-flavored cheese for more taste without having to use as much. Examples are parmesan, goat, feta, blue, Gouda, and sharp cheddar. I like shaving the cheese on top with a cheese shaver or even a potato peeler. It makes a nice, thin layer that covers a lot of surface.

Most salad dressings come with too much salt, sugar, fat, and other additives. You can eat salad dressings on the side and dip each forkful into it. Or, pour just two tablespoons of dressing onto your salad and mix it well to coat it entirely.

At restaurants, ask them to go light on the toppings or order them on the side. The quality of the toppings makes a difference in terms of how much needs to be used. For example, a bland, fake-cheese topping will require they add much more than if it were a high-quality cheese with an abundance of flavor. Not to mention, these fake toppings are usually loaded with salt and chemicals. If a vegetable comes to my table with too much cheese, oil, or salt, I send it back and ask for something else.

It may sound intimidating to ask a waiter to change your dish, but most waiters and chefs truly want their customers to be happy. They'll honor a request like this without a problem. Also remember, a restaurant is likely to make changes to their menu if they get enough requests from their customers. This is my motivation to speak up. Think of it as giving great data to the chefs and owners of the restaurant—in a nice way, of course.

Prep Fresh Vegetables Fast

To avoid foodborne illness and remove pesticides, we need to wash fresh vegetables. Fill a giant bowl with cold water, add a few drops of vinegar to kill any small bugs and germs, and let the vegetables soak for a few minutes while doing other things. After they've soaked, put them in a colander and rinse.

For a little extra money at the grocery store, you can buy fresh, precut vegetables to save time. To be safe, you'll want to wash these vegetables too. Avoid using vinegar on porous vegetables because the flavor will sink in.

These vegetables need no prep. You can simply wash and eat:

- dark greens

- carrots

- sugar snap peas

- ready-cut green beans

- grape tomatoes

- cucumbers

- red, yellow, and orange bell peppers (These don't cause gastric distress for some like green peppers do.)

These vegetables can be cooked in about five minutes by

stir-frying, grilling, or steaming:

- corn
- peppers
- green beans
- peas
- sugar snap peas
- asparagus
- zucchini
- eggplant
- bok choy
- mushrooms

Root vegetables are great roasted. These are typically cooked with lots of oil, but you don't need it. Simply put a very light coat of oil on the bottom of a baking pan. Stir the vegetables around to lightly coat them with the oil. Heat them in the oven for about 40 minutes at 350 degrees, turning them about halfway through. Try:

- squash
- turnips
- beets
- carrots
- Brussels sprouts
- sweet potatoes
- regular potatoes

Bags or clamshells of ready-to-eat dark greens are great. I use them many days of the week. They're great as a simple salad on the side of almost anything. I throw these eye- and brain-healthy greens into sandwiches and wraps or onto my pizza. And yes, pizza can be eaten in a healthy way! See chapter 4 for more on that.

If you like multitasking, here's one situation where it actually makes sense: while prepping vegetables, you can talk on the phone on speaker or a headset, catch up with your favorite podcast or TV show, or share your day with a family member. Just make sure to keep eyes on your knife.

Make It Happen

Something as easy as making up half of your lunch and dinner with vegetables will help you prevent illness, fight disease, reduce inflammation, protect your brain, and preserve your youthfulness and energy. Succeeding at this step will improve the way you feel and perform and greatly contribute to your optimal performance and longevity in leadership. Start thinking outside the box to reach your goals of eating more of these incredible foods so you can receive all their benefits. Once you start seeing and feeling the results, you'll be strongly motivated to keep going!

In the next chapter, we'll discuss the second half of the "most important thing" you can do for your diet. First, challenge yourself for a week to eat more delicious vegetables and make your new food experiences interesting and enjoyable. Gather data in the Dynamic Lifestyle Road Map. You're building a foundation for your very own, personal system that will enable you to eat for long-term success.

| CHAPTER 3 |
HAVING INTEGRITY AND STARTING YOUR DAY TO WIN

You've already succeeded in a big way. If you followed my advice, as of now, you're more than halfway to getting the recommended amount of plant food for optimal health. By eating three or more servings of vegetables per day in the way I recommend, you're adding an invaluable number of nutrients to your diet, as well as subtracting a large number of unnecessary calories. Plant foods play a critical role in optimizing your body and brain, sustaining your health, and supporting your energy to be a vibrant and vital leader long beyond your expectations.

After completing this chapter, you'll be getting even more than the daily recommended amounts. It's exciting because you can feel and see your body and performance improve with time as you eat these beneficial foods. I'll keep making it as simple as possible, and you'll keep taking the steps that make sense to you. Soon your new practices will become a habit and a natural part of your life. Before moving on, I want to ask you this important question:

Do You Have Integrity with Yourself?
Integrity is a fundamental pillar of good leadership and the foundation of all good relationships. Integrity means that you do what you say you're going to do, and you are who you say you are. When you have integrity in work and your relationships, you are someone people can count on and respect. Only then will they trust you enough to truly lead.

You may be practicing integrity in your work and with others, but do you have integrity with yourself? Are you someone who you can rely on, respect, and trust? When you say you're going to take better care of yourself, do you do it? For many leaders the answer is "no." Integrity stops where their relationship with themselves begins.

But we often forget that our success in leadership significantly depends on our health and energy. And these depend on how well we take care of ourselves. Lack of attention to our diet, not exercising, not getting enough sleep, and neglecting ourselves in general contributes to burnout and fatigue. When we're deficient in self-care, we end up with insufficient energy to make the best decisions, put our best foot forward, or put in the extra effort when it counts. Many times, we end up without the energy to be our best self when it really matters.

The practice of breaking promises to yourself has its own consequences. After making enough promises to yourself that you'll "do it tomorrow" without following through, each additional promise adds to your stress because you subconsciously know you won't honor it. The stress levels rise again when you beat yourself up for not following through.

It's important that you become the person you can trust the most when it comes to taking care of yourself, if you're not already. Besides reducing stress, there are countless benefits to this. One of which includes being a strong and resilient leader, with energy and stamina to conquer challenges in the best way possible as they arise.

Practice at least one of the activities I suggest in each chapter. Take action to the extent that you plan. If you haven't been doing that, it's a good time to start having more integrity with yourself. And now, onto the next step!

What and Why
Your first meal of the day needs to provide you with high-

quality fuel so you can be at your mental and physical best from the start. This is why we'll zero in on breakfasts and snacks in this step. You'll practice building easy, healthy, delicious food combinations during these mealtimes to energize your brain and your body during the earlier part of the day. These early meals, when done right, can help you avoid the afternoon slump and reduce your cravings for sugar, fat, and junk foods. They'll give you energy and stamina to conquer your morning challenges with finesse.

You may not eat breakfast, and that's okay. I've had clients who don't like breakfast, and I've never required anyone to eat it—everyone's body responds to food differently at different times. We'll call your first meal of the day "breakfast" no matter what time you eat it. But as you read through this chapter, you'll understand why eating food earlier in the day can be very beneficial.

In this step, along with three servings of vegetables per day, you'll focus on eating two to three servings of fruit per day. Fruits are the second part of the five-per-day minimum I mentioned in the last chapter. After this step, you'll be getting the full-on, recommended amounts of these plant foods so you can benefit from the phytonutrient power they offer.

Like vegetables, fruit is packed with fiber and water so it will fill you up with minimal calories and won't slow you down. Fruit is nutrient-dense, high in unique combinations of vitamins, minerals, antioxidants, and phytochemicals. Like vegetables, fruit has been proven to help fight inflammation, illness, and disease, keep your brain sharp, and even turn back the clock on aging—from your skin down to your DNA. All of this contributes to your energy and performance and your ability to be an excellent leader.

An Introduction to Nutrient Timing

Traditionally, the term "nutrient timing" is reserved for topics related to how an athlete eats before and after training and races to optimize results. But everyone can use nutrient timing to get a performance edge—both physically and mentally. So, let's talk about your nutrient timing in the morning and how you can make it work to optimize your energy for leadership.

First, think about this: How many hours pass from the time you eat dinner until you go to sleep? Add that to how many hours you sleep at night, and that's how many hours your body and brain have gone without food. You may have heard that breakfast got its name from the fact that we're actually breaking a fast. And you can see from your calculations that you have been fasting for some time overnight.

Add to your long nighttime hours without food the fact that your body and brain do some heavy work at night. During deep sleep, your human growth hormone (HGH) does most of its work. HGH is the hormone that keeps you looking and feeling young. Also, during sleep, your body repairs damage from injury, illness, stress, and pollutants, and rebuilds itself. It's especially important for recovery if you've done serious exercise that day. During sleep, your brain puts information from your day into long-term memory and sorts and organizes information in your memory banks. A lot goes on while you sleep, and it takes energy!

After we awake, we're transitioning our energy usage from evening repair and replenishment to whatever needs to get done first thing in the morning. As you recall from my introduction, executive functioning is an energy-demanding activity, and your brain works best when it's rested and fueled. You may now see how mornings are good times to refuel in order to set your day up for success.

Evidence has emerged that humans have a circadian rhythm when it comes to metabolism. The latest research shows that many of us have increased glucose tolerance, glucose sensitivity, and fatty acid oxidation earlier in the day versus the evening. Our system is primed to digest, absorb, and make energy out of our food earlier rather than later; it seems

63

best that we eat most of our food and calories during the day rather than in the evening. There's also evidence that having breakfast in the meal formula I'm suggesting in this book can lower risk for type 2 diabetes and metabolic syndrome because it can bolster your glucose metabolism for a significant time after eating it. It can even improve the metabolism of your next meal.

These are reasons to eat a meal relatively early in your day. If a traditional breakfast doesn't work for your body and your digestive system, don't force it. There are many creative ways to eat a little food in the morning so you can get the great benefits of breakfast. During this step, you'll experiment to find out what is your best "first" time to eat and what foods are best for you at that time. I'll help you figure it out.

How I Found the Right Combination of Food in the Morning

Unsweetened cereal used to be my breakfast while growing up. As an adult, boxes in my cupboard consisted of flakes made of whole wheat or corn, whole-grain Os, and sometimes puffed grains. But I never felt they gave me any energy. Sometimes after breakfast I'd feel even more tired. That wasn't helpful!

When I became more conscious of calories, I was amazed that the average three-quarters cup serving of unsweetened cereal was 100 calories. If I let myself eat until I was full, I could easily eat a whole box of cereal. That's about 1,000 calories of cereal without even adding milk.

Popular media may have you thinking that I didn't feel good after breakfast because of the milk. Or you may guess it was the carbohydrates in the cereal that were making me feel tired. It was a little of each but not for the reasons that the fads might have you believe.

I'll debunk some popular myths about carbohydrates and milk in future chapters, but for now, I'll give you this point: one of the biggest reasons eating boxed cereals wasn't doing me justice was because it wasn't a balanced meal. Here's how I accidentally fell into my answer to a better breakfast.

It was 7 a.m. on a weekday morning, and I was frantically looking for something to eat. I only had a few minutes to grab breakfast and get out the door. Unlike some, I don't function well without food in the morning.

Like most weekdays, my next chance to eat would be about 2 p.m., so food was imperative. I opened the cupboard to grab my whole-grain cereal box, and to my dismay—there was nothing! What to do? My schedule was booked solid, so I couldn't grab something on the way to work.

Facing the reality that I might need to guzzle some strong coffee and run on fumes for half the day, I found some oatmeal way in the back of my cupboard. It was neither quick nor instant. It was old-fashioned. I had bought it for making cookies at least 10 months ago.

I was in a rush and didn't have time to deal with pots and dishes. So, I made a bowl in the microwave. I knew it'd need some flavor, so I cut up an apple to sweeten it, threw in nuts for texture, and added milk to cool it down so I could eat fast. That combination turned out to be incredibly tasty with no added sugar needed! The best thing about it came later that day.

When I finally got to lunch seven hours later, my mind was still fully functional, and my body still felt strong. This was different from most days when I'd feel about ready to pass out right before lunch. I was shocked. Afterward, I experimented with oatmeal daily, and every day I worked from morning until 2 p.m. without an energy dip. I consistently had enough fuel to be on top of my game until much later than the average American lunchtime.

This is now my go-to breakfast. It's part of my morning system. With all other decisions on my mind in the mornings, what I'm having for breakfast is not one of them. I have the making of it down to a science, and it takes less than three minutes. I don't get bored with it because I change the fruit depending on the season.

Through experimentation, I found that this breakfast doesn't sustain my energy in the same way unless it has all four ingredients: whole-grain oatmeal, fruit, nuts, and milk. Contrary to the confusing media messages, it's not the protein or the fat or the carbohydrates that make you feel satisfied. It's the *combination* that makes the winning formula. The ingredients work together to help your body feel satisfied and fuller for longer and provide lasting energy to your brain. This breakfast has protein from milk, oatmeal, and nuts; healthy fat from nuts; complex longer-acting carbohydrates from unrefined oatmeal, nuts, and fruit; and simpler, faster-acting carbs from fruit and milk. The breakdown may seem confusing if you don't know how to categorize food into protein, complex carbs, simpler carbs, and fat. But by the end of your journey through this book you'll have a good idea about how to do that. And you'll be able to make these kinds of healthy, balanced meal choices on the fly like I did. Just stick with me and take this step by step.

Since we're experimenting with what works best for your breakfast, I encourage you to try my oatmeal combination this week to see what happens. If you're not an oatmeal person, it's okay! I've had plenty of clients who like egg breakfasts. Some people even like breakfasts that resemble lunch, which is more common in Europe. No matter what kind of breakfast you like, whether it's oatmeal, eggs, or a sandwich, in this step you'll be experimenting to discover your optimal breakfast. And you'll be experimenting with fruit in your breakfasts. You may have heard that fruit is high in sugar and you shouldn't be eating it. If that's the case, let me help liberate you from that myth!

Fruit Sugar vs. Added Sugar

It's true that Americans are eating too much sugar, and it likely contributes to some of the major health issues we currently face. In 2009, the American Heart Association released a scientific statement that excess added sugar can increase the risk of cardiovascular disease by increasing inflammation and raising triglycerides. It can also contribute to increasing your risk of obesity, insulin resistance, and type 2 diabetes. We also know that overeating sugar can make it addictive, causing you to want more of it, and need higher doses in order to taste it.

The sugar we're eating too much of in the U.S. is *added* sugar. This is where the danger lies. Most added sugar in processed food comes in the form of high fructose corn syrup (HFCS), which is made from corn starch and concentrated into sugar in a factory. Scientists are researching the independent harmful effects that overeating HFCS, in particular, may cause. The concentrated sugar of HFCS makes a liquid that's sweeter than sugar, is cheaper than sugar, and dissolves easily in any food—solid or liquid. This is how 10 teaspoons of sugar can be dissolved in a 12-oz. can of Coke!

The American Heart Association recommends that women eat less than 100 calories of added sugar per day (about 6 teaspoons), and men eat less than 150 calories (about 10 teaspoons) of added sugar per day. But people in the U.S. are consuming much more than that in the form of sugary snacks and drinks. Whether it be HFCS, white sugar, brown sugar, honey, or agave, it's all added sugar if it doesn't come naturally in a food. What's worse is that you'll find added sugar in processed foods and restaurant foods as a preservative, even in sauces, breads, and bagged and boxed foods that aren't sweet. Americans are getting overloaded with sugar without even knowing it.

Fructose in fruit is not the same as HFCS. Inside the fruit, molecules of fructose are bound to molecules of fiber and water. Your body has to work to separate the fructose from the fiber before it can absorb into your system. It is not the same as concentrated sugar, like HFCS, which absorbs quickly into your blood from your digestive system and can overload your blood with glucose, followed by insulin. This causes your energy levels to spike and then drop, which, as you might imagine, is disadvantageous for a leader or anyone who pushes their brain and body for long hours. The naturally occurring sugar in fruit takes longer to be released into your blood, and it gives a more gradual release of energy. It won't cause your blood sugar levels to spike like candy, soda, cake, or processed foods made with heaps of added sugar. Therefore, the sugar in fruit doesn't do the harm that eating loads of added sugar does.

In fact, the faster-acting, safe carbs in fruit provide energy that your brain and body can really use in the morning. And because of the fiber and water in fruit, you'll feel fuller and more satisfied when you eat fruit than when you eat candy or drink soda. Plus, you get all the unique and beneficial antioxidants, phytochemicals, vitamins, and minerals that fruit has to offer that contribute to an optimally functioning mind and body. In short, fruit is a good food!

A few years ago, I interviewed Dr. Robert H. Lustig, a pediatric physician, researcher, and author—one of the first to speak loudly about the dangers of eating too much added sugar. He wrote the book *FAT Chance: Beating the Odds Against Sugar, Processed Food, Obesity, and Disease*, and his speech at the University of California San Francisco about the dangers of HFCS went viral on the internet.

Unfortunately, there were some major misunderstandings derived from Dr. Lustig's message. One of the biggest was that fruit (with fructose) posed the same danger as HFCS that Dr. Lustig was speaking out against. Scores of people began giving up fruit and the natural benefits and energy that it provides, thinking that it was the same as HFCS. During our interview, Dr. Lustig confirmed that, contrary to popular belief, he wasn't suggesting that people avoid fruit.

Another myth perpetuated from the doctor's message was that HFCS is literally a poison. While Dr. Lustig has used the word "poison" to describe HFCS, he didn't mean that if you have a small amount of it in your hot sauce or salad dressing a couple of times per week it's going to cause you to die! But rather, it is dangerous and may cause serious physical problems that can shorten your life if you constantly overload your system with added HFCS—like the American population is doing today. If you'd like to see this interview, which has many more interesting points from Dr. Lustig, I've provided the web address in the references for this chapter (see Gabel, 2017).

How do we avoid the detriments of HFCS and added sugar in general? Eat fruit more often than desserts, sweet treats, and sweetened coffee drinks. Avoid soda as much as possible and drink more water. Eat more real food and less processed food. And save the desserts that are disguised as breakfast foods, like doughnuts, coffee cake, nut and banana breads, croissants, bagels, muffins, pancakes, and waffles for special occasions.

Step 3—Starting Your Day to Win

Here's how to proceed with this step:

1. Make fruit half of every breakfast and snack. Each time you eat fruit, eat at least one serving. Similar to vegetables, I've made serving sizes simple and easy to remember. A serving of fruit here is:

• One large piece or one cup of fruit. For small berries, like blueberries, a serving is a half-cup.

• Like vegetables, you can use your entire closed fist to approximate a cup-sized serving.

2. Like vegetables, eat fruit in its simplest, most natural, and whole form. In other words, eat pure fruit the way you find it in nature. We'll call this "clean fruit." This means eat fruit with as few toppings and additions as possible. For example, eat it without sugar, whipped cream, or ice cream on top. Eat your fruit fresh, rather than canned or processed. And eat dried fruit infrequently, because without water, the sugar in the fruit

becomes concentrated. Given a little time, you'll begin to appreciate the real flavor of whole fruit, and you'll start to become more sensitive to the natural sweetness it has to offer.

3. Diversify. Like vegetables, every fruit has its own signature combination of nutrients and benefits. Eat different fruits with different colors during the day to get your widest range of natural vitamins, minerals, antioxidants, and phytochemicals for optimal mental and physical health and performance.

4. Pay attention to how your first meal of the day makes you feel and how much energy it gives you. Journal in the Dynamic Lifestyle Road Map so you have good, hard data on how this meal is working for you and what could be changed for the better.

5. Continue filling half of your lunches and dinners with vegetables. Now, half of every meal will be either fruit or vegetables or both. When you do this, you'll be getting the minimum and likely more than the recommended amounts of fruit and vegetables that's been scientifically proven time and again to provide all those "miraculous" benefits to your body and brain.

Now, your meal proportions look like this:

Judi's Story

We're circling back to Judi, the entrepreneur and mom of two. Wondering why she craved cookies and ice cream so much she asked, "Why didn't nature make it so I crave food that's good for me rather than sweets or junk food?" I told her that there's an assumption that a desire for sweets is in our genes because toxic foods tend to be sour or bitter. Therefore, humans attracted to a sweet taste had a better chance of surviving and not getting poisoned, so the sweet-tooth gene was passed on.

More importantly, we crave simple carbs when we need energy. Simpler carbohydrates digest quickly, get into the blood, and head right to the places that need it most, like our muscles and our brain. Our sweet craving is doing what it's meant to do: telling us that our blood sugar is low and needs to be elevated fast—or else.

Research in neuroscience has shown that our blood-sugar level affects our ability to think. A boost of sugar when we're running low on energy will cause an uptick in our brain's ability to perform. It's why many office workers get hooked on soda and highly sweetened coffee and tea drinks.

Caffeine and sugar are one way to keep the brain going, but we don't have to answer the craving with junk food or sugary coffee. It makes much more sense to have natural, nutrient-dense fruit instead of processed, calorie-dense food when your body needs that boost of energy. And you can combine fruit with any meal to take advantage of its faster-acting energy when you need it.

The thing about having sugary, processed food or sweetened drinks for a quick pick-me-up is that—sure, they'll elevate your blood sugar fast and help you feel a fast energy boost—but without having real food and fiber in your system to control the sugar release into your blood and keep your energy going, your blood sugar will drop right back down again just as fast. Most often, it'll leave you in a worse energy slump than before you ate. I'll share more on that in the next chapter.

After Judi observed her body and documented her food for a short time, she realized that in most instances when she craved sugar, she hadn't had a meal in over five hours. So, she shifted her habit from having cookies and coffee to eating a small meal (assembled in the way I'm sharing) at that time instead. Along with her weight loss, most of her sugar cravings and afternoon slumps had disappeared. She was able to cruise into the evening and have more energy for quality time with her children. She wasn't on a miracle diet, she wasn't taking expensive supplements, and she didn't have to do anything drastic. She just started eating the way her body was meant to eat.

Judi had been putting off taking care of herself for years with the excuse that there were too many other things to do. She realized that she hadn't had integrity with herself for a long time: Caring for herself and family with healthy food was a value of hers that she'd been neglecting. What she didn't know was that her three-year-old son had been observing her eating habits and modeling her. One day, he started asking for fruit instead of cookies before dinner. He wanted to eat like Mom. She was delighted.

It's Your Choice

Here are ways you can work this step into your everyday life. Choose a couple that resonate with you and stretch yourself a little.

1. Swap it. Since fruit is naturally sweet and packed with a powerful punch of vital nutrients, see if you can enjoy it in place of sweet snacks you typically eat during the day.

2. Experiment with it. Use fruit as a sweetener instead of sugar, honey, or sugar substitutes.

3. Front-load it. If you typically crave sweets after a meal, try eating fruit *before* your meal. Sometimes we wait too long to eat between meals. By the time we get to dinner, our blood sugar can be so low that we barely have the energy to make a

good decision about food, let alone make a meal.

After eating a meal, it may take time for your blood sugar to increase and for you to feel energized again. If you boost your blood sugar with fruit on your way home from the office or while making dinner, you may find you no longer crave dessert afterward. If that doesn't curb your sugar craving and you end up eating dessert, I'm betting you'll eat much less of it because you'll have satisfied your needs with real food first.

Maximize Your Opportunity for Success

Here are some common questions I get about this topic.

Why the emphasis on fruit for morning meals and snacks?

It's simple. (Pun intended!) Because fruit offers simpler, more readily available carbohydrates along with fiber and vitamins; it's very helpful when your blood sugar needs a quick but safe boost, like in the morning or at snack time. Fruit requires less prep, so it's good for eating on busy mornings, and it's easy to pack and snack on during the day.

Can I eat more vegetables instead of adding fruit?

Yes, as long as you're eating *two* more servings in the amounts recommended above, and it adds up to a total of five servings. But try to eat some fruit for its complementary nutrition.

Can I have more than two servings of fruit per day?

Yes. The more fruits and vegetables you eat in a day, the better. And you'll most likely be displacing other, less- healthy foods.

Does fruit on the bottom of yogurt count as one serving?

Fruit at the bottom of yogurt is essentially jelly. And jelly or jam doesn't count as fruit because it's full of *added* sugar. In fact, count jams and jellies as sugar.

Does juice count?

Drinking juice or a blended drink doesn't offer the same benefits as eating fruit. In addition, like soda, fruit juice can give you a fast overload of sugar. For that reason, I don't recommend drinking juice regularly. It's better to eat your fruit. "See Juice It, Blend It, or Eat It?" in The Leading Edge section for more.

Acknowledge Yourself

Positive acknowledgment is a powerful way to motivate people and reinforce good work. Acknowledging *yourself* is equally powerful and motivating. Leaders typically don't have many opportunities to receive positive feedback from others. Therefore it will be good for you to get into the habit of recognizing your own successes: Acknowledge yourself for keeping your promises to yourself regarding your food choices. Congratulate yourself for succeeding at any of the food goals you set for yourself. It takes only a moment, and it creates lasting, positive effects.

If you don't know how to do that, here's a good way to start: imagine what you'd say to an employee, a coworker, or even your best friend. You might even think about what you'd say to one of your children after they've accomplished something great. Then, in your mind, say it to yourself. Try it now and see what I mean. Practice regularly.

THE LEADING EDGE OF SUCCESS

These extra details will give you an edge when it comes to succeeding in each step. You can read it all or choose the topics that interest you most.

Smart Morning Coffee Drinking

If you're a coffee drinker, try having a little food in the morning before your first sip of coffee. You may be surprised at how much breakfast helps to wake you up. You may even find you don't need as much coffee as you've been drinking. Eating food before your first cup of coffee can also help you avoid that afternoon slump. Because you're not getting a false start with caffeine and avoiding food, which is the real fuel.

A caffeine buzz will hide your hunger. If you have coffee before eating breakfast, it'll hide your body's desire for food. And when the caffeine wears off and you don't have any blood sugar left, you'll crash. The longer you've gone without food, the lower your blood sugar will go and the harder you'll crash.

We can "fake-fuel" our body with caffeine all the way through the day, which is what many clients of mine did for years before working with me. They drank caffeine in the morning until the afternoon crash, had very little food at lunch with another large serving of caffeine, and then one more caffeine jolt to get from 3 p.m. until the end of the workday. The problems with that are: (a) they avoid giving their body and brain the food and nutrients they need for optimal performance, (b) they developed a tolerance to the caffeine so they needed to drink more and more to feel the kick, and (c) years of "fake-fueling" with caffeine and eating very little real food ended up extremely compromising their metabolism, sleep, mood, and mental capacity—all of which I'll expand on in the next chapters.

On the other hand, you can use nutrient timing and capitalize on the fact that caffeine reduces hunger by drinking coffee the European way. In many European countries, it's customary to have a small serving of coffee or tea after a meal. This small dose of caffeine can take the edge off temptations to get dessert or overeat. That dose of caffeine can also extend your satisfaction and energy from food. And since having a meal helps us relax, if it's not yet time for you to relax, the caffeine will keep you revved. An espresso is nice after meals because it doesn't take up much room in your stomach.

I recommend avoiding caffeine or any other stimulant-containing drink in the evening, so it doesn't compromise your sleep. Herbal teas and water with ginger, mint, and/or honey can be very enjoyable in the evening.

Afternoon Slumps and the Carb-Crash Cycle

The midday crash, also known as the afternoon slump, is most often caused by a blood sugar dip. It's a common problem. As you already know, when you're running low on blood sugar, your brain is less capable of making good decisions. Along with having a detrimental effect on your work, it can lead to making less-than-optimal food decisions. Most of the time, during the afternoon slump, people will eat whatever's in front of them— be it coffee cake, candy, or a sugar-loaded coffee drink. And those aren't good solutions.

Not only are we loading the wrong kinds of food into our system, we're also opening the door to what I call the *carb-crash cycle*. When the caffeine and the simple carbohydrate that you ate for a fast snack wear off and there's no long-term fuel in your system to pull you through, you'll have another crash. The *after-work danger zone* I spoke of in chapter 2 is often the second part of a crash cycle that starts with an afternoon slump that isn't remedied with real food: the simple-carbohydrate, processed food wears off and sends you into another crash before dinner. A crash cycle is tough to break. Usually, you have to sleep it off and start over again the next day.

Juice It, Blend It, or Eat It?

Since we're talking about morning food and fruit, you may think it's a good idea to start drinking juice or smoothies in the morning. I advise against it. Drinking juice isn't the same as eating fruit.

Even though there are vitamins in fruit, believe it or not, a glass of fruit juice provides almost as much sugar as a glass of soda. When you separate the juice from pulp and fiber, you get a more concentrated sugar drink. It's not as concentrated as HFCS but definitely more than the original fruit. Since you don't have to chew it, it doesn't take your digestive system much work to digest. The sugar gets into your blood much faster than it does with natural fruit. For that reason, juice can cause a similar blood sugar spike as candy, cake, and soda. You'll also get that unfortunate blood sugar crash afterward, and that's not ideal.

Blending your fruit instead of juicing it is a little better because you'll still drink the fiber. But the fiber has been partially broken down by the blender and your body doesn't have to work as hard to digest it either, so the sugar will still be absorbed faster. In addition, like Jon in Chapter 1, because you're drinking instead of eating food that takes time to digest, you can drink hundreds of calories and still feel hungry in an hour or less. Even though you'll get a lot of vitamins from drinking all that fruit in one glass, most of us can't afford to down all those calories without feeling like we've eaten.

On the other hand, drinks made in a blender are an option if you need to get more calories or nutrients than your regular meals offer, or if there are no other healthy food choices. The healthiest blended juice is made with mostly vegetables and a little fruit added for sweetener.

Smoothie establishments are very popular. The serving sizes of these drinks are often so big that the calorie content is much higher than any reasonable snack. To add to the problem, they frequently come with added sugar in the form of syrup, ice cream, coconut flakes, tapioca, or other sweet treats. The calories go up again if you add protein powder. Anything over a size small can pack five hundred to a thousand calories or more into a drink. They're another way to accidentally consume more calories than you need. I probably don't need to tell you these are not fruit servings—at best, they're desserts. When you do have one, make it a small size!

Five-Star Restaurant Secrets

In this section, we're deconstructing the five-star plate. Using these secrets, you can put together incredibly tasty meals with ease at home or anywhere you find yourself. In the last chapter, we discussed using simple, fresh ingredients to optimize taste. The next secret is the following: incorporate a few contrasting flavors in your meal to excite your taste buds and bring the enjoyment of your meal to another level. When your mouth is satisfied with exciting flavors, your brain will be more satisfied too. You'll be less likely to feel like you need "a little something" after dinner to round out your meal. Here are some examples:

1. Sweet and bitter tastes go well together. For example, you can make this kind of contrast in a dark green salad with fresh fruit. The following are a few salads that come to mind: spinach with strawberries, mangoes, or nectarines; kale with raspberries, blackberries, or blueberries; and arugula or mixed greens with peaches, pears, or apples. Any combination of the above will create a salad that tastes exciting and exotic.

2. Another one of my favorite combinations is plain pizza (Margherita style) with arugula (bitter greens) piled on top and a drizzle of balsamic vinegar reduction (sweet) over the whole thing.

3. Umami is an earthy flavor, similar to mushrooms or meat. Combine umami-flavored foods with bright and sweet vegetables like carrots, red or yellow bell peppers, or green sugar snap peas. Fruit like oranges, tangerines, mangoes, or pineapple taste great in a stir-fry with chicken, beef, or seafood.

4. Sweet and savory flavors are also contrasting. Add fruit to a cheese or vegetable tray for a superb balance of tastes. Add apples or pears to the top of a chicken or turkey sandwich for some sweet, crunchy excitement.

Fruit and Table Sugar Don't Mix

Fruit sugar has a very different taste from table sugar. When you add table sugar to fruit, the fruit will taste much less sweet!

You'll need to add a lot more table sugar than you might have expected for the sugar to take over what will now taste like a bitter fruit. This is the case with fresh, uncooked fruit as well as with jam, compote, or pie filling. It's why jams and jellies are mostly sugar.

You can avoid the whole problem by relying on the natural sweetness of the fruit without adding sugar. Most fruits have a wine-like flavor with a little tartness. Like wine, it's an acquired taste but once you get there, you'll really enjoy it.

Creative Ways to Eat Real Fruit

• Store fruit at work for quick, easy energy. Keep longer-lasting fruit in a desk drawer or your car for quick snacks.

• Put fruit into your breakfast bowls for sweetener.

• Have fruit instead of hash browns on the side of an omelet.

• Have fruit instead of chips on the side of your sandwich.

• Add fruit to plain yogurt instead of eating presweetened yogurt, where the fruit is just jam incognito.

• Have a bowl of fruit for a simple dessert. Berries are sweet and tart, like a glass of wine. Baked apples sprinkled with cinnamon are great in winter.

• Instead of dressing, try fresh-squeezed citrus fruit on salad with a little olive oil. Lemon or lime is fun and uplifting. When in season, fresh peach or mango juice is incredibly good.

• Add any fruit to dark green salads for complementary flavors and a dash of exciting color.

How to Curb Your Sweet Tooth

Do you love sweets, like me? If so, I've got great news—you can curb your sweet tooth. You've already started your first big step toward success with this. By focusing on eating healthy foods and regularly getting well-balanced meals, you've already started to prevent blood sugar dips, afternoon slumps, and brain fog. This will help reduce your cravings for sugar and other junk food in a big way.

If you still find yourself staring at that package of sweets, here's a tip on how to curb your appetite for it before you eat it:

1. Check the nutrition information on the package and find out, according to the manufacturer, how much of that sweet food makes up a serving.

2. Next, see how many grams of sugar are in that serving.

3. A teaspoon of sugar has about 4 grams of sugar. So, divide the total grams of sugar in a serving by 4 to find out how many teaspoons of sugar you're about to eat. Imagine yourself sitting down to eat that many teaspoons of sugar at one time.

Knowledge is power. With that knowledge you can decide whether you want to eat a whole serving or less, or none at all! This practice has helped my clients and me eat much less sugar.

Simple Carbs and Nutrient Timing

Many athletes will grab simple sugar, like candy, cookies, or even a cupcake, right before a race. That's because simple carbs provide immediate fuel. They'll process fast and get out of the digestive system and into the blood faster than any other food, with no bulk in their belly to slow them down. It's the opposite of how most people want to feel after a meal, and it works for this situation.

In fact, protein, fat, and fiber will not work right before a hard training session because they all take too long to digest. If you start to run or jump with undigested food in your stomach, it can be a recipe for disaster. You may not even get the workout you were counting on if things get bad enough! So, simpler carbs have a function immediately before a hard workout, race, or training session, when fast fuel is needed.

They can also be useful after a workout if you're not expecting to eat for a while. Athletes know that replenishing blood glucose after a workout stimulates insulin, which stops your muscles from breaking down (catabolism) and starts them on the road to recovery (anabolism). The sooner you can eat and increase your blood sugar after a workout, especially if it was intense, the better results you'll get. It's important for you as a leader, because it'll help you feel less tired and sore, have more energy, and even maintain a better mood afterward. But rather than simple carbs like sweets or pastries, a meal made in the way I'm suggesting in this book will always be your best option for post-workout recovery. It'll give you both immediate, and longer-lasting, steady blood sugar.

When you're in the office and need a fast blood sugar boost, a far better choice is fruit. A banana, apple, or orange is not the same as candy or soda, coffee cake, or a croissant. The fiber you're eating with any fresh fruit will slow the feed of sugar into your blood and prevent the big uptick in blood sugar and subsequent crash that comes with eating man-made, sugar-laden foods. It won't take you through a race, but it'll save you until you can get to a meal or well-rounded snack. Equally important is the fact that you're getting a bounty of other nutrients that will benefit your body and brain.

In any case, emergency low blood sugar situations are something leaders want to avoid. Leaders need to be highly functional and on top of their game for 10, 12, sometimes 14 hours per day. This is why you want to find the right combination of food and the best times to eat it. As far as exercise is concerned, you can time your meals for eating an hour or so before exercise, so you have the power and energy you'll need for workouts, without requiring simple sugar immediately beforehand.

Alcohol
Alcohol falls into the sugar category. Like sugar, it has nothing

to offer you but empty calories; if you drink it on an empty stomach, it can produce a blood sugar crash that can make you moody or sleepy. And like sugar, extra calories from alcohol turn into body fat. In the case of alcohol, some of that fat can place itself on your liver and internal organs, which can cause serious illness in the long run. When you drink alcohol, treat it like dessert: have small amounts after you've eaten real food. At the very least, have a glass with food, not by itself, to slow its uptake into your body and brain. There are many ways wine or beer can add dimension to a meal. But it needs to be consumed in moderation and with mindfulness because it is a drug and a non-nutritive substance.

Be Uncompromising with Your Self-Integrity

Be uncompromising with your self-integrity to succeed at these food goals. Your first meal of the day, when done right, will get you up and running with even-keeled blood sugar levels to power your brain and body for optimal performance long into the afternoon. In fact, you can have even-keeled energy all day if you want it, which happens to be the subject of the next step.

First, give yourself a week to experiment with breakfasts and fruit to find out how you can best start your day with energy. Experiment with the snacks you eat as well, including fruit to see if it can help keep your energy going. Journal in your Dietary Lifestyle Road Map and start exploring your personal nutrient timing needs. You're creating your personal food system for success, and you want to create a system that works—and lasts!

| CHAPTER 4 |
BALANCING YOUR ENERGY THROUGH THE DAY

If you implement only what you've started in the last three chapters for the rest of your life, you'll be setting yourself up for having above-average quality of life, longevity, mental capacity, and physical health. It will help you be a more resilient and capable leader and lead much further into the future.

Unbelievably simple steps can dramatically improve your health; curtail illness; reduce your weight; help you look, feel, and perform like a younger version of yourself; live longer; and improve your mental focus and energy. Right now, you're on track to have this amazing health, vitality, and energy for years to come in ways that you may not have thought possible.

Leaders Need an Exceptional Amount of Energy

For most people, energy is elusive. It's something that comes and goes. If they're lucky, they have it when they need it. But leaders can't take that chance. Leaders need to have endless streams of energy. As a leader, you need energy for productivity. You need energy to motivate, inspire, and compel others to action. You need to be in a positive mindset and mood all day, or at least whenever you're around others. And you need to make decisions and take action all day, often into the night. Together, these add up to mental and physical demands over and above what comes naturally to most people. So, you need to develop as many support systems as possible for the high levels of energy you demand of yourself.

We tend to forget that food is the source of energy for our body and mind. Caffeinated drinks are often our go-to fix when we need energy. But wouldn't it be ideal if we could eat to have even-keeled energy that lasts? Wouldn't it be even better if food could somehow also help us get sleep when we need sleep, be awake when we need to be awake, have better moods, be more patient, fuel our immune system, and feel stronger and more competent overall? I'm here to tell you, it's not only ideal, it's possible.

What and Why

In the last two steps, you worked on filling half of your breakfasts, lunches, dinners, and snacks with fruit or vegetables. Now you'll focus on the next part of your balanced meal system, one that plays an important role in regulating your energy: carbohydrates, also known as carbs.

We started our carb conversation in the last step, and now we'll expand on it. There's a lot of conflicting information about carbs in the media today. On the one hand, you'll hear that vegetarianism is the healthiest way to eat. Vegetarianism includes eating beans, grains, and vegetables, which are all carbohydrate-dense foods. On the other hand, you'll hear that avoiding carbohydrates and eating more meat and fat is the healthiest way to go. And there's all the advice in between.

The answer is not as black and white as popular trends make it seem. In this step, you'll discover in greater detail what carbohydrates are and how your body and brain use them. You'll also experiment with nutrient-timing tips regarding how you can use carbs to optimize your immediate and long-term energy. You'll find out for yourself how much you need, which carbs work best for your body, and what times are best for you to eat them. One thing we know is that we need carbohydrates. And they have benefits you don't want to miss.

What Do We Need Carbs for?

Leaders need fuel to power through long and challenging days. Our bodies and brains use one of the simplest carbohydrates of all for fuel: glucose. You're using glucose right now because you're using your muscles to sit or hold yourself upright, your eyes to see, and your brain to process this information and think. All this requires energy provided by glucose. Glucose also maintains all your unconscious body processes, like your heartbeat, digestion, and immune system. It's the fuel for *all* our cells.

The term "blood *glucose*" is interchangeable with "blood *sugar*;" however, blood glucose is not the same as the table sugar we eat, which is a combination of glucose and fructose. Glucose is the technical name for the simple carbohydrate that floats in our blood and is not as sweet.

What Are Carbohydrates Anyway?

All foods have a combination of nutrients. You can find some amounts of carbohydrates, protein, and fat in almost every food. But we call some foods "carbs," others "proteins," and other "fats" based on their predominant nutrient.

Carbohydrates come in different forms. They're all molecules made up of carbon, hydrogen, and oxygen strung together in a chain. Some are short chains that we call "simple carbs," and some are long chains that we call "complex carbs." Simple and complex carbs come in a variety of combinations in most foods.

Sweeteners like table sugar, agave, honey, fructose, sucrose, brown sugar, and others are primarily made up of short-chain carbohydrates, also called simple carbs. Because they're simple, they don't take much energy to digest, and they move quickly from your digestive system into your blood. Foods made predominantly of simple carbs, like cakes, cookies, sodas, and other sweets, are low in nutrient density; they have very few nutrients and their main contribution to our diet is calories.

These easy-to-digest carbohydrates, when eaten alone, will cause an uptick in your blood sugar. It's not healthy for blood glucose levels to be too high for too long. So, when our blood sugar levels go up from sweets our body will put any excess sugar in our blood—that's not used immediately—into storage. Places where we store excess glucose are muscles, liver, and fat, in that order.

Foods made of more complex carbohydrates take more time to digest. The longer and more complex the carbohydrate chains are, the longer it takes your digestive system to pull it apart and turn it into glucose. Little by little, a complex carb is broken down by digestion, and small amounts of glucose are fed into the blood. This gives you a longer, slower release of energy, which is just what you need. These carbs don't dump an excess of sugar into your blood at once. Rather, they provide a longer-lasting burn of energy, longer-lasting fuel, and more stable blood sugar levels for longer time periods. These are carbs that are not processed, such as vegetables and fruit, potatoes, yams, legume beans, and corn and other whole grains in their whole form.

The most complex carbohydrate is fiber. Most fiber doesn't get broken down or absorbed into your blood. Essentially, it passes right through you. But because of the way it passes through, it helps to clean your digestive tract. One of the most recent findings on fiber is that the beneficial bacteria in our gut (our gut microbiome) eat it and are sustained by it. Those who don't eat enough fiber have a fragile gut microbiome that is prone to illness and digestive problems. See "The Secret Benefits of Fiber" in The Leading Edge section for more details.

That's it. There is nothing inherently bad about carbs, like many fads want you to believe. They're organic molecules and part of what makes life on earth. They're also necessary and beneficial. I created The Carbohydrate Spectrum™ to help you easily understand the different kinds of foods in which you'll find various types of carbohydrates. Take a look at it when you get to The Leading Edge section.

Should You Be Eliminating Carbs from Your Diet?

Fad diets today suggest that you eat fewer carbohydrates and more fat. They're called low-carb or high-fat diets. They'll ask you to eat between 50%–90% of your calories from fat. The ketogenic diet is the highest-fat diet, which suggests you get up to 90% of your calories from fat.

Are diets like this right for you and your energy as a leader? You'll be able to decide for yourself after reading this chapter. But it's very difficult not to eat carbohydrates. There are three macronutrients that we get calories (or energy) from: protein, carbs, and fat. If you eat zero carbs, you have to be eating only protein and fat. And that means no fruit and no vegetables, and that's no good.

Almost all plant food is composed mainly of carbohydrates. Plants are where we get most of our antioxidants, vitamins and minerals, and they're our only source of phytochemicals. We can't avoid carbs completely and still have an optimally functioning body and brain. Even meat has some carbohydrates in it. It's called muscle glycogen, and I'll share more on that soon. So, what do people mean when they say they're "not eating carbs?" Most of the time, they're using the terminology incorrectly. At this point, you know too much about nutrition to make that kind of mistake.

Not eating enough of the right kind of carbs can lead to low blood sugar. Do you remember the last time you had low energy caused by low blood sugar (aka low blood glucose)? Let me give you some examples of how it can affect you in the short-term.

Short-Term Dangers of Low Blood Sugar

Since our brain functions on glucose, when our blood glucose levels get low, our brain is affected. Operating on low blood glucose isn't ideal for anyone who wants to be a good leader. It has consequences on your energy as well as your ability to relate to people, be patient, maintain a good mood, and communicate. Here are some ways research has shown low blood sugar can affect your brain:

- It becomes difficult to make good decisions.

- It gets harder to put thoughts into words.

- You might feel sad and depressed; you might even feel like you want to cry.

- You can become impatient, easily agitated, or angry.

- You can become unusually anxious.

- You might get migraines.

- You can feel unusually tired.

- You can become light-headed and dizzy, to the point of feeling off-balance, or feel like you're going to pass out.

On top of the negative effects low blood sugar can have on your brain, it's not great for your health or your weight. You'll remember from the last chapter that we crave simple carbohydrates when our blood sugar gets low. We crave them because they're the foods that absorb quickly into our bloodstream and give our cells the emergency boost they're looking for. Since low blood sugar hinders our ability to make good decisions and weakens our willpower, it's hard to resist foods like cake, cookies, chocolate, sweet coffee drinks, soda, pretzels, and chips when our blood glucose drops. If we allow our blood sugar to get too low too often, we may soon see our body weight go up due to extra body fat.

The Risks of Eating Too Few Carbs Long-Term

Even if you don't feel the short-term effects of low blood sugar, not eating the right amount of carbohydrates for your needs can be harmful in the long-term. Research shows that the body thinks it's starving when it doesn't get enough carbs. This affects our stress hormones and metabolism in complex ways. For example, when you go for long periods without enough

carbs, you risk having:
- increased levels of the stress hormone cortisol
- decreased thyroid levels (T3) and slowed metabolism
- lower testosterone
- reduced ability to build and keep muscle
- a compromised immune system

The increase in stress hormones can lower fertility, increase inflammation, and increase body fat. If you're a female, a reduction of thyroid hormone can mimic early menopause, cause hair loss, dry skin, and dry mucous membranes. And a combination of these effects can cause loss of bone. Since women are already predisposed to increased rates of bone loss after the age of 30, we don't need to speed that up!

You should also be aware that carbohydrates stimulate the production of serotonin and dopamine—hormones that reduce pain and help us relax and feel happy. Psychological studies have found that a deficit of carbs over time can increase depression, anxiety, agitation, and anger. It can also have a detrimental effect on sleep. It's probably easy now for you to see how all of this can have a significant, negative impact on your ability to work well with others and can ultimately undermine your efforts to be a true leader.

Sleep and Carbohydrates—My Story

It was 3 a.m. in Italy and I was standing in the living room of my in-law's apartment, staring out the window at the darkness. I had jet lag. But at that time in my life, I had been having problems falling asleep and staying asleep past 3 a.m. regularly. So, this was nothing new. On most nights, I'd just get up and work.

That night, I decided to have breakfast before getting on my computer. I made my signature oatmeal and got ready to get some early morning work done. To my surprise, my body started to relax. In about half an hour, I went back to bed and slept deeply for the next three hours. What a surprise that was.

After that event, I started noting my eating patterns as they related to my sleep. I found that my middle of the night wake-ups were related to whether I had enough carbs for dinner that evening. As it turns out, the low-carb hype in the media was getting to me, and I had been eating less of them.

Through journaling and observation, I found that if I don't get enough carbs at my evening meal, I wake up after three or four hours and can't fall back to sleep. It's not good, because it's four to five hours less sleep than sleep experts say we need for optimal brain function and physical repair.

By taking notes on my meals, I figured out how much of each carbohydrate-dense food I'd need to eat at dinnertime to sleep through the night. After that, my whole life shifted. I unexpectedly eliminated the migraine headaches that had been waking me in the middle of the night for the previous 5 years. My injuries, when I had them, hurt less in the middle of the night. Of course, I was less tired because I was sleeping well. But most importantly, I felt like my brain was given a turbocharge; I had fewer energy slumps during the day, I could think more clearly, remember important details readily, and the right words came easier to me when speaking.

My story is just one example of how not eating enough carbohydrates can interfere with your sleep and how that affects so many other aspects of life. Many people have shared with me that they don't sleep as much as they need, and they walk around tired most of the time. Many of these same people have bought into the "life-hacking" advice that we can function optimally on less than seven to eight hours of sleep. These sleepless victims are usually also dealing with multiple, complex physical aches and pains, and weight that they can't lose. I usually find out they're also on some kind of low-carb diet. It's a catch-22 of not eating the right foods, not being able to sleep to repair and reset the body and mind and having the physical and mental issues that come from both.

Carbohydrate-containing foods aren't "bad" like popular fads of today will lead you to believe. But there are better and worse ways to eat them. You'll understand how to use carbohydrates to your advantage—for sleep and other benefits—by the end of this chapter.

Step 4—Balancing Your Energy Throughout the Day

In this step, you'll be experimenting with the kinds of carbohydrates you eat, how much you eat, and the best time to eat them. The carbs you'll be eating regularly in meals are what I'll call "carb-dense" foods. There are carbs in these foods that are easier to digest and absorb than fiber but not as easy to digest or as fast-acting as simple carbs. These are the carbs that will give your body and brain long-lasting, even-keeled energy. Many of these also have the gut-cleansing, immune-boosting, inflammation-fighting properties of plant food. Here's how to begin:

1. Make one quarter of your meals and snacks high-quality, carb-dense food. To make it simple, here's what we'll call a serving:

• One cup of cooked grains in their most natural, unprocessed state. This includes grains like corn, oats, rice, barley, farro, buckwheat, quinoa, oatmeal, and all others.

• One medium-sized (or one cup of) carbohydrate-dense vegetable. This includes yams and potatoes of all kinds. Speaking of potatoes, there is some serious misinformation circulating about them that may have made you question eating them. If so, I've got answers for you in The Leading Edge section.

• Similar to the last steps, you can use the size of your closed fist to estimate a cup.

• Pasta and pizza can be one of your carb-dense foods. This is when you eat them in their cleanest, healthiest forms, and portion them in your meal the way I'm outlining here.

You'll find more details in The Leading Edge section about how, and in what forms, pasta and pizza can have a place in a healthy leader's diet.

Unlike vegetables and fruits where your goal was to eat *at least* one or two servings with every meal, in this exercise, you'll start with a serving per meal and work up or down from there. Because of their nutrient density, vegetables and fruits can be eaten in a limitless fashion. But the foods that fall into the categories we call "carbs," "proteins," and "fats" contain more calories in general, and for that reason, everyone needs different amounts.

You'll do well if you keep your meals in the proportions I'm recommending. If you're more active or have a larger body size, you'll need more food in general. If you eat more food, keep the same ratio of carb-dense foods to vegetables. If you're a smaller person and eat less food, you'll need smaller portions all around. As you pay attention to what you eat, you'll discover whether more or less is needed. A food app can come in handy here too.

From now on, you can assume I'm referring to carb-dense food when I talk about the "carbs" section of your meal. You can visualize your meal proportions like this:

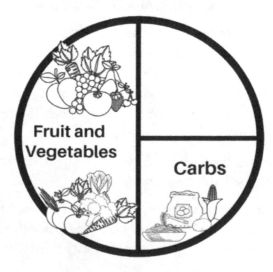

2. Eat all your carb-dense foods in a clean way, just like you've been doing with fruits and vegetables. Go very light on the oil, butter, cheese, cream, sour cream, bacon, salt, and sugar. Experiment here and see if you can taste the natural flavor of good, healthy, energizing food without unnecessary alterations that can leave you feeling heavy, slow, and tired.

3. Redefine your vegetables. As you may have noticed, now you'll include carb-dense vegetables like potatoes and yams in the carbohydrate quarter of your meals. Corn is a grain and belongs there too. You'll keep the lighter, more watery vegetables in the vegetable portion of your meal.

4. Diversify your carbs too. Rotate your carbs just like you rotate your vegetables and fruit. The more variety and diversity you get into your diet, the more likely you'll get the broad range of nutrients that the different carbohydrate sources have to offer. Keeping a highly varied diet will also help you avoid food sensitivities or deficiencies that can come from eating the same type of food over and over.

5. Experiment with the amount of carb-dense foods you eat daily and the times you eat them. Maybe a serving per meal is too much for you; maybe it's not enough. Keep track in your personal Dietary Lifestyle Road Map so you can get some data and make your best, most informed decisions about this energy-providing food.

Losing Weight with Low-Carb Diets—Denis' Story

Have you been influenced by the high-fat, low-carb diets even just a little? If so, you may be a little nervous about this step. After all, so many people in social media and magazines have sworn their allegiance to low-carb diets because of how much better they feel and how much weight they've been able to lose in a short amount of time.

It's just more misinformation and confusion caused by media and marketing. You'll soon understand why we can lose weight fast and feel different when we drastically restrict carbohydrates. The easiest way for me to explain is with a little story about my husband and his friends.

My husband is the opposite of me when it comes to his sensitivity to blood sugar. He can go for days without food if he needs to. Whereas, I'm so sensitive to small blood sugar swings that I can go from "feeling fine" to "feeling faint" within minutes if I wait too long for food.

I'm not sure whether Denis' superhuman ability to go for so long without food is genetic or because he's trained his body to be that way. You see, Denis has been a competitive, semiprofessional athlete for about 15 years. As a Judo and Jiu-Jitsu competitor, losing weight for competitions is a big part of his life. He's got it down to a science. His fastest weight loss ever was 11 pounds in three hours.

Before I share a couple of his secrets to fast weight loss, I'll tell you that Denis and his competitive peers already walk around with low body fat. When it comes time to lose weight, they don't have a lot of fat to lose, but they can drop between 10 to 30 pounds pretty quickly.

Denis is an aerospace engineer. He doesn't have all day to dedicate to exercising or making and eating special foods for a special diet. His friends also have full-time jobs and families. So, how do they do it? Of course, they lose the little fat they have, but the rest is what I call "weight manipulation," which is one of the secrets to how low-carb diets work.

Weight Manipulation—Dieting Like an Athlete

Your muscles are the largest carbohydrate storage area in your body. They absorb glucose from your blood and keep it on reserve for when they need it. They're efficient about it too. They'll take those short-chain glucose molecules and pack them into long, compact chains called muscle glycogen. And for every gram of glycogen, your muscle stores about 3 grams of water. This helps your muscles to have the food and water they need close at hand, so when the brain tells them to move, they can respond quickly.

If we exercise regularly, our muscles get the hint that they'll be needing fuel on a regular basis, and they get even better at absorbing glucose from the blood. In fact, the more muscle you have, the better you'll be at regulating your blood glucose. Many of my clients have improved their blood sugar regulation after strength training and building more muscle. It works so well that building muscle can even curb a diabetic's need for insulin.

Regarding the athletes, toward the end of a weight-loss cycle, these guys are eating only protein and watery fruits and vegetables. As they continue to exercise and avoid all carbohydrate-rich sources of food except undigestible fiber, their muscles get depleted of glycogen and the water that's stored with it. Since every gram of muscle glycogen is attached to about three times its weight in water, it makes for very fast weight loss.

The guys I'm talking about here are fit, healthy, and full of energy. Yet, they feel terrible and sluggish, and even cranky, when they're depleted of carbohydrates. This is definitely not how a leader wants to be feeling.

I've spoken to many athletes who diet for competition, and they'll be the first to tell you that this kind of diet is not what people should be doing for a lifetime. You can watch my interview with Denis and his teammate, Jeremy Jackson, and get more of their secrets about weight loss and eating for optimal performance in the video *Losing Weight Fast, Two Athletes Tell All*, listed in the References (Gabel, 2017.).

It doesn't matter if you're athletic or not; athletes are great specimens of the human body under extreme conditions. Leaders have their own set of extreme conditions. The point of the story is that if you've been on a low-carb diet, you may not realize how much better you can feel, and how much more energy you can have, if you ate the right kind of carbohydrate foods regularly.

Maybe you've heard about people who can exercise intensely, even complete marathons on high-fat, low-carbohydrate diets. Studies show that about 2% of people can reach very high levels of activity without eating much carbohydrate, while another 2% are on the other side of the curve and need more carbohydrates than most. Most people fall somewhere in the middle of the bell curve.

Some clients of mine have said, "But if I eat one serving of carbohydrates, I'll put on two pounds!" Are they exaggerating? Sometimes yes, but sometimes they're not.

If we deprive our body of carbs, when we start to eat them again, our weight can go up immediately. Because like the athletes on a low-carb diet, you're walking around with muscles depleted of glycogen and water. If we've been starving our muscles for fuel for so long, what do you think they'll do when they finally get the opportunity to store up some energy? You can bet they'll suck it up and hold onto it, so they have it when they need it. Carb depletion isn't the body's favorite state to be in.

When these athletes have their first meal with carbs after a competition, they can put on pounds in minutes. It's just starving muscles absorbing what they need to be optimal. If you were on a low-carb diet and decide to experiment with eating carbs again, don't get worried if you see the numbers on the scale go up. Let your muscles restock on fuel. As long as you're eating healthy carbs and the right portions, you'll be okay.

It's critical to remember that the scale doesn't tell the whole picture of your health; it doesn't separate fat from muscle, bone, blood, or body water. If you haven't already measured your body fat, it's a good idea to do so before you start experimenting with carbohydrates. And pay attention to all the other measurements you recorded in Step 1 of your Dynamic Lifestyle Road Map. These will give you the whole picture of how your body is faring when you feed it the right kinds of carbohydrates.

A great benefit is that you'll be recording your energy levels and other general changes in how you feel when you eat carb-dense foods this week. Keep your eye on the prize, which is conquering your day with more mental and physical energy, being more productive, having regular good moods, and sleeping well. As an extra bonus, you'll have the energy you need to be more active. Maybe you'll even take on a little more exercise. All of this together contributes to a longer life with sustained vitality and endurance to be the kind of leader you want to be. Loss of body fat typically comes along with it.

Why Some People Feel Better on Low-Carb Diets

In my experience with all kinds of clients, I've observed a big reason why some people feel better on a low-carb diet is because of one major thing: they've eliminated junk food. For so many people, not eating "carbs" means no cookies, cake, candy, cheap pizza, pretzels, chips, loaded baked potatoes, Pop-Tarts®, sugary cereals, sweet breads, French fries, and more. Get the picture? When you take out all the carbohydrate-rich food you eat, you'll certainly take out the junk food that was making you unhealthy, tired, and moody in the first place. In addition, as you may remember from previous chapters, most diets increase your intake of fruits and vegetables in some way. Vegetables and fruit are the secret to diet success. They're also a big reason why many physical ailments disappear.

There have been some excellent studies that have compared fat loss between low-fat/high-carb and high-fat/low-carb diets. The findings were predictable: the reason why people lose body fat on either of these is the same reason why people lose fat on any diet—they ultimately eat less calories overall.

Finally, MSGs, salt, sugar, and other preservatives can be hidden in your food in large quantities, and they're usually packed into that processed junk food that's made out of carbs.

These can cause your body to hold onto water, produce fast weight gain, and make you feel bloated and lethargic. It's not the best way to feel when we're performing leadership activities all day. So, for best results, eat clean carbs and eat them in the right proportions.

It's Your Choice

The goal here isn't that you stop eating all your favorite foods that contain carbs but that you start choosing the healthiest forms of them as possible, so you can get the benefits they offer. Start from where you are and stretch a bit. Here are some ways to work on this step this week:

1. Choose better when eating out. If you eat out at restaurants all the time, begin choosing carbohydrates in a healthier way. For example:

- Nut breads, banana breads, muffins, pastries, pancakes, and doughnuts are in the same category as cake. Have them infrequently, not as your everyday breakfast or snack.

- Eat a baked potato instead of fries, and when you do, have fewer toppings. Eat one topping instead of three or five. You might even try light salad dressing on your potato, or plain yogurt, instead of sour cream or butter.

- Eat baked chips or, have carrots or a cut apple with your meal if you're looking for that crunchy texture.

- Eat a whole-grain wrap or whole-grain bread when you eat a sandwich. Steer clear of sandwiches made with white bread the size of your calf.

- Avoid having pasta as a main course. Pasta isn't inherently bad for you, but it's not good when it's the biggest part of the meal and served with few, if any, other nutrient-dense foods. Instead, have a side of pasta along with the other foods I'm suggesting here. Share the pasta with others if there's enough to go around.

• Get pizza from a place that can be trusted to use real, whole-food ingredients rather than heaping on processed meats, fake cheeses, and questionable oil. (More on that in The Leading Edge.)

2. Take control. If you'd like to be in greater control of what you're putting into your body, pick one or two days per week to make meals at home. You'll avoid processed, questionable ingredients, and the inordinate number of calories that most restaurants sneak into popular carbohydrate dishes. If you're not ready to make an entire meal for yourself quite yet, grab a protein dish from your favorite restaurant and add your own vegetables and carbs at home. Carbs are so fast and easy to make—I've put details on that in The Leading Edge section. Be sure to make extra food for lunch the next day or keep it in the fridge for another fast and easy-access meal in the next couple of days.

3. Fine-tune things. If you're already doing all of the above, make the carbohydrates you are eating even healthier this week by using less cheese, butter, salt, and processed sauces. Keep refining the way you eat carbs, when you eat them, and how much you eat.

Maximize Your Opportunity for Success

There are so many ways you can leverage your knowledge of carbohydrates to evade the myths, avoid any detriments, and maximize their benefits. Take advantage of The Leading Edge information at the end of this chapter to expand your knowledge and skills in choosing the right carbs and the right amount at the right time. Be sure to look at the Carbohydrate Spectrum™ and Carb-Activity Spectrum™, which will help you to get an even better grasp on how to eat carbs for your benefit.

Acknowledge Yourself

If you add carb-dense foods in the proportions I suggest this week, you'll be adding another nutrition boost to your diet that will help your body and brain perform better. And you'll be increasing your nutrient density and cutting down on your calories again without even trying. Remember that any small change you make for the better in your diet is compounded over time, and you'll notice more benefits as you continue.

You can fortify yourself for being an excellent leader. And when you do, you'll make a big difference in your life as well as the lives of many others. Acknowledge yourself for doing what it takes to make this happen.

THE LEADING EDGE OF SUCCESS

These extra details will give you an edge when it comes to succeeding in each step. You can read it all or choose the topics that interest you most.

What Happens When We Don't Get the Sleep We Need?

Despite all the proponents of "sleep hacking," sleep research still upholds that the human body needs seven and a half to eight hours of sleep each night to be optimal. We need to look at the big picture and what happens over time when our body doesn't get the sleep it needs.

Lack of sleep can:

• impair attention, alertness, concentration, reasoning, and problem-solving

• increase your risk of heart attack, stroke, and diabetes

• kill your sex drive

• make you forgetful

• cause irritability and depression

• make your body gain weight and hold on to weight

- compromise your immune system

- cause early outward signs of aging

Your leadership capacity will greatly benefit from full doses of sleep at night. One test to see whether you're getting enough sleep: if you can't be functional at all in the morning without having coffee first, it's highly likely you're not getting enough sleep. In chapter 2, I asked you to experiment with having at least a little breakfast before drinking your first cup of coffee in the morning so that you can feel the energy that food can give. You'll be most in tune with the energy you get from food when your body gets enough sleep.

The Secret Benefits of Fiber

Fiber is the most complex carbohydrate of all. It's so complex that much of it can't be broken down by our digestive system. For that reason, the calories from fiber don't get absorbed. This is one situation where the calories truly don't count! Fiber adds bulk to food and causes us to feel fuller with fewer calories. For most people, most of the time, that's a good thing.

Cutting-edge research finds that the microbiome bacteria in our intestines feed off fiber from fruit, vegetables, and grains. The more beneficial fiber we eat, the healthier our microbiome is. This translates into better digestion, better immunity, less inflammation, fewer physical aches and pains, and more tolerance for all kinds of foods. Emerging evidence reveals a healthy microbiome is involved in helping us maintain a healthy weight and is related to our mental health as well.

There are two kinds of fiber: soluble and insoluble. Think of insoluble fiber like an edible scouring pad that's softer and kinder to your intestines; instead of cleaning dishes, it cleans your intestines from the inside as it moves through them. Insoluble fiber is abundant in all whole grains, fruits, and vegetables—basically, all plants.

Soluble fiber is different. It combines with water in your

digestive system and creates a gel. This gel also cleans your intestines, only this one absorbs fat and cholesterol as it moves through. This is why oatmeal is one of the few foods that can actually claim to help reduce cholesterol—because of its soluble fiber. Not many foods have soluble fiber. Foods other than oatmeal include lentils, kidney beans, chickpeas, green peas, barley, and carrots. Nuts, seeds, and citrus fruit have some soluble fiber but in much smaller amounts.

When you eat high-fiber foods as part of a meal, you lower the speed at which all the other foods, and the simpler sugars from those foods, are absorbed. This is specifically how fiber helps you maintain normal blood sugar levels. When you eat fiber-containing foods each time you eat, the energy from your food will last longer, your energy dips will be less intense, and you'll have fewer of them throughout the day.

The Carbohydrate Spectrum™

To the Left:	To the Right:
• Simplest carbs	• Most complex carbs
• More calorie-dense	• More nutrient-dense

After much research and thought, I created this spectrum to summarize the wide variety of carbohydrates and where they're found in food. This is to help you be better equipped to use carbohydrates as a tool—to fuel your energy when you need it, in the way that you need it. Match the numbers on the scale with the descriptions below.

1. The simplest carbs are sweeteners (like agave, honey, maple syrup, and table sugar). All sugars, no matter where they come from, have the same effect on the body. Also in this category are foods made up of mostly sugar such as sodas, candy, and jams. Many fruit juices are also in this category. These are the foods containing the simplest sugars that digest quickly, get into your bloodstream fast, and increase your blood sugar levels. These sugars need to be used at once, or your body will put them into storage for later, that being primarily muscle or fat.

2. Next, there are the processed foods made with white flour *and* added sugar. These are sweets like muffins, cake, cookies, and sweet "breads," which are really just cake. Most energy bars, even though they may have some whole grains or nuts, are filled with sugar. These cause similar blood sugar spikes as the items in number one above, and the energy they give you won't last long.

3. Breads and cereals that aren't sweet may not have as much added sugar, but because they are highly processed, their carbohydrates are simple. The processing of grain into white flour removes the outer covering of the grain (the hull), which contains most of the beneficial fiber. This makes the grain a simpler carbohydrate (also known as *refined grain*). It's another product that gets quickly into the blood. These foods can also cause a blood sugar "spike" leading to an energy slump if we eat too much of them at once or without other, nutrient-dense foods to slow their digestion and absorption.

4. Some whole-grain, processed foods are better than others and fall farther to the right of the spectrum. The best way to know where your processed-grain food falls on the spectrum is to read the ingredients list. On packages in the United States, ingredients are listed in order of their predominance: the ingredients used in the greatest amount are listed first, followed in descending order by those used in

smaller amounts. If a product is truly made mostly of whole grains, you'll see "whole grain" at the top of the list. This means the fiber hasn't been removed. But to make a dough with whole grains, they still need to be ground down into flour. So, ultimately, they will digest faster and pass through your digestive system faster than if you ate the actual grain itself.

5. Fruit has simpler carbohydrates that are entangled in plenty of fiber to slow their uptake into your blood. However, fruit provides a faster source of fuel than other complex carbs. All fruit is high in nutrients and low in calories.

6. Next are the carbohydrate-dense plant foods with a combination of fiber as well as complex, longer-chain carbs that we can absorb and digest. These are yams, potatoes, and whole grains like corn, wheat, rice, quinoa, farro, and more. To a smaller extent, carrots, beets, parsnips, peas, beans, and legumes have this readily available carbohydrate and even more insoluble fiber, which puts them closer to number seven on this spectrum. These carbs offer more fuel for your body and brain that is slowly released into your blood as your digestive system breaks it down. They have high levels of nutrients—vitamins, minerals, phytochemicals, antioxidants, and so on—so their nutrient density is high. They also provide more energy.

7. Finally, at the far right, we have leafy and watery vegetables where most of the carbs are essentially undigestible, insoluble fiber. They have very high-nutrient density and very low-calorie density, so they don't provide much energy. But they do have plenty of vitamins, minerals, and phytochemicals, as well as water.

The Carb-Activity Spectrum™
How much carbohydrate do *you* need?

To the left of center are those who:

Are less active

Have less muscle mass

Do more sitting throughout the day

Therefore:

Need fewer calories and fewer carbs for muscle glycogen

Watery fruits and vegetables can be sufficient

To the right of center are those who:

Spend more time being active, do more intense activity, or both

Have more muscle mass

Do less sitting throughout the day

Therefore:

Need more calories and more carbs for muscle glycogen

Need more carb-dense foods

Most of us need to eat some of the denser-carbohydrate sources to get the amount of energy our body and brain need to perform optimally without crashing. The amount and kind of carbohydrate you need depends on many things, including your activity level, your body size, your metabolism, and the amount of muscle you have.

I created this Carb-Activity Spectrum™ as a visual aid for understanding your carbohydrate needs. If you're someone who sits a lot or maintains a low level of activity, you're probably going to fall more to the left of the spectrum. If this is the case, you can feel completely fine and energized if you eat fewer carbs or if the only carbs you eat are from watery fruits and vegetables. The more active you are and the more muscle you carry, the more carbohydrates your body will want and need. You'll find your carb needs are farther to the right of the scale and you'll need more carb-dense foods.

Some people's bodies are much more sensitive to carbs and need more carbs to function optimally. Some are less sensitive and don't need as much to function optimally. If you aren't eating the right amount of carbohydrates, your body can signal you in the following ways:

- You feel hungry even after eating a meal.

- You don't have enough energy for workouts and other physical activities.

- You aren't recovering from your workouts.

- You're not sleeping well at night.

- You have unusual bad moods.

- You're not thinking well.

- You have constant cravings for sweets, chips, pretzels, or other junk-type foods that are simple carbohydrates.

How We Gain Five Pounds in Two Days

Do you ever think you gained five pounds of fat over the weekend? It's important to remember that we gain body fat slowly because of the large number of calories you need to eat over and above your requirement. It's why most people's body fat creeps up over the years. There are approximately 3,500 calories in a pound of fat. Granted, it's not that simple; everyone's metabolism is slightly different when it comes to how many calories get absorbed and stored from our food. But in general, it helps to remember that the number of calories that add a pound of fat to the body is large and it will take some time to do.

Think of it this way: fat is our most efficient, physical storage of calories. It's intended to be our emergency fuel during times of famine. Because there are 9 calories in a gram of fat and only 4 calories in a gram of carbohydrates or protein—it's a great way to store double the number of calories on our bodies for later. You'd probably know if you ate enough calories to gain a pound or more in a day or a weekend. If you don't think you'd know, then it could be a good time to log into an app to get a better idea of the calories in the foods you eat.

If weight loss is something you're looking for, by simply following my suggestions here and cleaning up your diet for better energy, you will start to see that happening without a diet. Fat weight loss takes time, but people succeed at it.

If you don't lose weight as fast as the athletes I spoke of earlier or like some of the contestants on popular weight-loss TV shows, it's not because you're failing. Just like fat comes on slowly, it also comes off slowly. When you lose 5 pounds in 2 days or 10 pounds in a week, it's highly likely that most of it is water and muscle glycogen. For more motivation on weight loss, watch my video, "How People Lose Weight and Keep It Off." You'll find the web address in the References.

Eat Pasta and Pizza Like the Mediterraneans

The Mediterranean diet has won awards for the healthiest diet in the world for many years now. In my travels to the Mediterranean, I've observed how pasta, potatoes, bread, and pizza are a perfectly healthy part of the diet. The people there remain some of the healthiest on the planet.

Many think it's a mystery that people in European countries can eat these kinds of carbs on a daily basis and stay as thin as they do. But in Italy, if you eat with the locals (not at tourist restaurants), you'll see that they're served differently from what we're used to in the United States.

When you order pasta at a U.S. restaurant, chances are you'll get a portion as large as a bed pillow, and it'll come with loads of sauce, likely containing sugar in the form of HFCS. It might be topped with imitation cheese and maybe even overrun with oil. To top it off, you'll probably get nothing but bread on the side of your pasta. In Italian restaurants that haven't been influenced by American food culture, pasta servings are the size of a fist, and vegetables and protein are considered equally important parts of the meal.

Another big secret to Italian eating is that traditional Italian chefs use only the freshest, most natural ingredients. It's something they pride themselves on. Italian pizza in Italy is made with fresh, real cheese and tomato sauce. It's never imitation ingredients like you'll find on some of the pizza we have in the United States.

French fries in France are served in smaller portions and with much less oil. These servings are about the size of your hand, with 15 to 20 fries total. If you put a few fries from an average U.S. restaurant on a napkin, there'll often be so much extra oil that in a few seconds it'll saturate the napkin. If you eat fries at a cafe in France and do the same thing, you'll likely not see any oil markings at all on the napkin.

Many French eat baguettes daily; Italians also eat bread, and the Spanish on the Mediterranean coast eat potatoes regularly. But many of the healthy French, Italian, and Spanish that you hear about still value very much making and eating food at home with family. The food they eat has fewer questionable ingredients and fewer calories in general. Eating large amounts of fresh vegetables and fruit is also part of their everyday lifestyle.

You *can* eat pasta, pizza, and potatoes and maintain excellent health. The caveats are that you (a) portion them according to this system, (b) eat them like everything else—in their most natural state possible with only the healthiest ingredients, and (c) if you eat them at restaurants, you do it infrequently.

No matter where you are in the world, you can create a healthy meal by choosing the right portion sizes and choosing foods made in the healthiest way, like I'm discussing here.

Can Carbs Make You Tired?

Many people tell me they feel tired after eating carbs and assume it's either because they're having an allergic reaction or because there's something inherently bad about carbs. But people also feel tired when they eat too much protein or fat. If we eat too much of any food, it can overload our digestive system and make us uncomfortable and tired.

As previously mentioned, carbs can help you relax. If you eat carbs in smaller amounts and in proportions that resemble the meals I'm recommending, this problem should be eliminated. Unfortunately, with restaurants serving up pasta, pizza, and rice in oversized portions, it's too easy to eat too much. Not to mention, these dishes are often loaded with heavy sauces, butter, and cheese, which will also give you post-meal fatigue.

Are Potatoes Healthy or Not?

Like many foods, potatoes have had their ups and downs in the media. The truth is that potatoes in and of themselves are a healthy food. They're a vegetable that comes with vitamins and minerals like calcium, iron, and vitamin B6. They're also high in vitamin C, which is an antioxidant that protects your cells and builds and repairs collagen, bones, and cartilage. All potatoes are low in sodium and good sources of potassium, which helps lower blood pressure, helps your muscles to relax, and reduces cramping.

What makes potatoes unhealthy is the way they're eaten. According to the U.S. National Potato Statistical Yearbook of 2019, 55% of the potatoes eaten in the U.S. are eaten as French fries, and 21% are eaten as potato chips. That means 76% of potatoes are eaten as junk food!

The average medium baked potato (2.25 inches to 3.25 inches in diameter) is 161 calories with 2 calories from fat, 4 grams of protein and 6 grams of fiber. On the other hand, a medium order of American fast-food French fries has 360 calories and 180 calories from fat—all from questionable cooking oil and a lot of added sodium. Another unhealthy way to make them is to top them with a mound of full-fat sour cream, a chunk of butter, heaps of bacon bits, and a pile of questionable cheese.

Another trendy misconception is that sweet potatoes are better for you than all other potatoes—this is not the case. The only major differences you'll find between the sweet potato and white potato are that sweet potatoes are loaded with vitamin A (438% of the daily recommended amount) and are higher in natural sugar than white potatoes.

Making Healthy Carbs Fast and Easy

Cooking carbs doesn't take a lot of time. Healthy carbs can be as easy as a microwaved potato; blanched corn on the cob, which takes three minutes in boiling water; or boiled pasta, which takes 3 to 10 minutes. Grains can be simmered in a pot while you remain productive doing other things, and a rice cooker cooks almost any grain without needing to be watched or timed. Most carbohydrate-rich vegetables can be microwaved or roasted in the oven.

Here are a couple more ideas on how to make carbs healthier at home:

• Replace boxed cereal with old-fashioned oatmeal or another whole grain like buckwheat or brown rice and top it with fruit and nuts.

• Eat potatoes with low-fat sour cream, plain yogurt, or even a light salad dressing instead of butter, cheese, and bacon.

• Eat baked potatoes instead of fries.

• Put a tablespoon of fresh olive oil onto your pasta instead of butter or cream sauce.

• Blanch fresh corn on the cob for three minutes in boiling

water to save the taste and texture. Try eating it without butter or salt to allow the full flavor to come through. It's delicious!

Five-Star Restaurant Secrets

Your meals can taste like you're eating at a five-star restaurant no matter where you are if you know how to put them together. The next five-star restaurant tip is to include contrasting textures in each meal. Multiple textures make a meal more pleasing to your mouth and increase your enjoyment and satisfaction of a meal.

A testament to this secret is the rise in popularity of meal bowls. These are typically combinations of a soft protein, crunchy fresh vegetables, and chewy whole grains all thrown into a large bowl with some sauce. Places selling these bowls are popping up all over major cities, and the recipes are popular online. People love bowls because they offer an exciting combination of texture, color, and taste with every forkful, and they're easy to transport.

When putting a meal together for yourself, use the same concept—combine different textures, colors, and tastes for high satisfaction and interest value. Try mixing it all together in a bowl with some dressing for a fun, completely different experience of the same food.

Will Eating Carbohydrates Help You Be a Better Leader?

If you don't know the answer yet, I'll reinforce it with an emphatic *yes!* Eating the *right* carbs will give you the energy to keep going throughout the day. They help you feel fuller and more satisfied with your meal for longer and will keep your blood sugar levels cruising in the normal zone for a long time. They'll help you get better sleep, and they're intricately involved in keeping a healthy balance of your hormones and your mood. All of this will help you make better decisions, be more productive, and be a better people-person. The right kinds of carbohydrates will keep your calories down and your cholesterol in check. They'll support your immune system and your gut microbiome. If you're a leader who exercises, and you absolutely should be, they'll supply you with energy to exercise harder and get more results from your workouts. Record some data in your Dynamic Lifestyle Road Map as you experiment with the best carbohydrates to eat and the best times to eat them. Your even-keeled mental and physical energy will have a positive effect on everything you do. In the next chapter, we'll focus on your mental and physical strength.

| CHAPTER 5 |
YOUR VISION AND HOW YOU LOOK, FEEL, AND PERFORM

I applaud your commitment to making habit changes for the better. It's not easy to stick with dietary changes. If it were, everyone would have a healthy diet. Of course, there are ups and downs on the road to changing habits, just like there are on the road to any other goal. Everyone falls off course occasionally. So, if you happen to fall off course somewhere down the road, just bring yourself back. Keep coming back, time and again, and you'll be very happy with your results. Those that stay on the path despite the ups and downs, are the ones who succeed in a big way.

Leadership and Vision

No doubt you've heard that success isn't determined by how many times you fall off your path but how many times you get back on track. What will keep you getting back on track over and over again? It starts with your deepest desires and dreams—the "Big Why" you identified at the beginning of your journey here. After that, it's your vision of achieving those dreams that will keep you motivated to continue moving forward.

Leaders have a high level of motivation and drive that's kept alive by big dreams and goals, and a vision of the future that inspires not only themselves but others as well. Great leaders are known for investing time and energy in nurturing their visions of the future. Athletes have been using visualization to perfect their game and win medals for decades.

Visualization is a tool for success that's at your disposal as well.

There are many psychological reasons for the fact that if you can see it in your mind's eye, you're more likely to turn your goal into reality. There's great value in allowing yourself some time to dream and visualize your goals being achieved in a future that inspires you. If you're not doing it already, it's high time you start practicing and getting the benefits.

To practice visualization, I suggest you take a few quiet moments each day to envision not only your goals and achievements and how they'll affect the world but also who you'll be in the world. As if you're watching yourself in a movie, envision yourself with optimal health and a brain that's sharp as a tack, making great decisions, standing tall and strong, feeling full of energy. See yourself enjoying your life, work, and the people around you. Picture yourself successfully making healthy choices. Envision yourself as the type of leader and person that you respect and admire. There's space in the Dynamic Lifestyle Road Map to write out some of your visions. A strong vision will help you stay mentally strong and resilient and motivate you to stay on your path, making good choices for the long run. It will help you achieve your goals and dreams, and inspire others, too.

What and Why

While on the topic of strength and resilience, it's a good time to discuss protein. Protein can affect your physical and mental resilience. It affects your health and leadership ability, too. As with carbs, you'll see that protein foods are not categorically healthy or unhealthy, but some choices are much healthier than others. I'll help you put knowledge into practice and choose the healthiest protein foods possible. And I'll dispel a few myths about this macronutrient.

What Is Protein and Why Do We Need It?

In simplest terms, protein is a chain of molecules called amino acids. Different from carbohydrates, protein has a basic structure that not only includes carbon and hydrogen but also includes nitrogen. We need protein for building and maintaining muscles, cartilage, bones, blood, and skin. Healthy muscles and bones give you structure, help you stand up straight, and make you look and feel strong. Let's be honest—perception is reality to most people. As leaders, if we look strong and capable, it's more likely that we'll be perceived as such.

If we do nothing to prevent it, our body starts to lose muscle after the age of 30 at a rapid rate. This is a phenomenon called sarcopenia. It's a big deal because when we lose muscle, we lose the metabolism that goes with it, which is largely responsible for keeping our body fat down. We also lose the blood sugar regulation that we get from muscle. When we lose muscle, we lose our youthful stature. We also lose physical power and our sense of power right along with it. Much of what we associate with an aging body is related to loss of muscle and our ability to perform the way we used to.

But we can keep our muscle, strength and stature, healthy blood sugar regulation, and metabolism. We can avoid sarcopenia if we (a) eat the right foods to keep our muscle and build more, and (b) exercise to stimulate our muscles to build in the first place.

Our body doesn't use protein for energy unless it absolutely needs to. This usually happens when we don't get enough calories for long periods. When the body starts using protein for energy, it also starts breaking down our muscles for calories. This is why it's recommended that we eat more protein if we're on a low-calorie diet.

Protein isn't just for muscle mass. Our body uses amino acids to build the microscopic structures that are involved in all our cellular functions. Amino acids build hormones and enzymes and the antibodies of our immune system. Amino acids make up neurotransmitters, the chemicals that provide the signals that travel between all the nerves of our body. These neurotransmitters are literally what makes our brain activity happen.

Dr. Lisa Mosconi, author of *Brain Food*, neuroscientist and associate director of the Alzheimer's Prevention Clinic in New York, says neurotransmitters "are actually produced each and every time there is a need to carry one of the brain's various messages. This is intrinsically dependent on nutrients extracted from the foods we eat day after day." Along with carbohydrates, the brain needs adequate amounts of amino acids to function at its best.

The brain and body can make some amino acids. These are conveniently called nonessential amino acids. Others can't be made. These are essential amino acids, and we need to eat protein to get them in adequate amounts for our brain and body to function optimally. Although protein deficiency isn't common in developed countries, there are two neuro-transmitters I'd like to talk about that are dependent on essential amino acids and are particularly related to leadership activity.

Serotonin

Serotonin is made from the essential amino acid tryptophan. It's the neurotransmitter associated with good moods and your ability to relax and be happy. It affects your sleep, emotional stability, and memory. It also plays a role in appetite regulation.

As a leader, you know the importance of relaxation to bring down your stress levels so you can recharge. When we relax, we restore our creative energy. We then have an easier time thinking outside the box and solving problems.

When we relax, we bring our cortisol (stress hormone) levels down. This allows more energy to be devoted to our immune system, giving it a better opportunity to do its job: fighting illness. When we're relaxed, we sleep easier at night, our digestive system functions better, even our reproductive system works better.

Dr. Mosconi shares that low serotonin levels in the brain can reduce the frequency and length of our feelings of happiness. Long-term, reduced serotonin levels can lead to depression and anxiety. And serotonin depletion has been associated with aspects of memory decline seen in advanced aging and dementia. I probably don't need to point out how maintaining good moods, avoiding anxiety and depression, and having a good memory is critical for good leadership for the long-term.

Dopamine

Dopamine, often referred to as the happy hormone, is a neurotransmitter involved with motivation, pleasure, and reward. It's an ingredient in adrenaline, the hormone that helps you get excited, and its counterpart norepinephrine, which helps you calm down.

Dopamine is strongly associated with your ability to pay attention and problem-solve. Our prefrontal cortex (the executive functioning area of the brain) is intensely supplied with dopamine. It also plays a big role in motor control—the control of your body movements. For this reason, it follows that abnormalities in dopamine are found to be involved in Parkinson's disease as well as ADHD. The creation of dopamine in the human brain requires phenylalanine, another essential amino acid.

We need protein for many functions. And there are just too many confusing messages about protein in the media today. On the one hand, you'll hear that animal protein can cause early death and an increased risk of cancer, so we should eat only plants. On the other hand, you'll hear that animal protein is best, and we should eat it in copious amounts. But what's real?

From my continued study up to this point, I can confidently say that eating healthy protein doesn't necessarily require that you avoid all meat, or avoid all red meat, or all chicken or all eggs. But it's important you know how to separate the healthy from the unhealthy and get the beneficial nutrients from protein without overexposing yourself to its potential hazards. I'll be helping you with that. I'll also help you understand how to get the most protein possible from a variety of different sources. I'll touch on how to approach vegetarianism in a healthy way. And I'll share how you can be kinder to animals and promote their welfare, even if you choose to eat meat. But first, here's an embarrassing little story of how disorganized I was about my own protein choices when I first began my career!

The Importance of Protein—My Story

When I was living and working in New York City, I was mostly a vegetarian, eating a piece of chicken about once every four weeks. I didn't want to eat animals, and I especially avoided red meat and eggs because of the detrimental health effects I'd heard about.

At this time in my life, I was always tired. I worked long days that started way too early for me. I was exercising regularly, lifting weights, and running. But I wasn't seeing the results I thought I should from my workouts.

I also wasn't organized with food. As far as I was concerned, eating wasn't something that should require thought or planning. After all, it's a daily life skill, like putting on clothes before work—it comes naturally, right? Just like I selected my clothes in the morning depending on my mood, what I ate when I was hungry depended on my mood as well.

I'd shop almost every night after work at the local deli. I didn't think about the time I'd save in travel, shopping, standing in line, and paying at the checkout by purchasing more than one meal at a time. I didn't know about the money I'd save if I bought food in larger quantities. I was also not aware of the better return I'd get on my time investment if I prepared multiple meals at once. But that wasn't my biggest problem, because I wasn't making the right food decisions in the first place.

My choices were based on not only what I felt like eating but also on what I could make fast. I started the morning with either a bagel and cream cheese or a bag of cinnamon raisin quick-style oats. For lunch, I'd have a salad or fruit. After lunch, I'd be so tired, I wished I could sleep for the rest of the day.

I ate pasta with red sauce for dinner about four nights per week because it was fast and inexpensive. At least once per week, I ate vegetarian Chinese food. Some nights, I'd have a potato or squash with broccoli. That was basically my repertoire of meals.

I was being as healthy as I knew how to be. I didn't eat pizza or processed or fried food. I wasn't eating much in terms of volume either. In fact, I was often hungry. I was strength training and running regularly, but my body still didn't look or feel like I thought it should with all the work I was putting into it. I was working hard at being optimally healthy, but I wasn't successful because I didn't know that I was missing something.

After New York, I went to Seoul, South Korea, where I was in charge of developing a health club and spa for the Department of Defense. I turned a mid-sized health and racquet club into a large club with a pool, juice bar, retail store, and additional amenities. I oversaw the entire operation with 90 staff and several managers as direct reports. The job took up my whole life at the time. I had no food plan and no food in my refrigerator, so I ate breakfast, lunch, and dinner out regularly.

Most nights, exhausted after work, I'd order food from the adjacent hotel. I maintained my habit of eating pasta with red sauce and a salad for dinner. When eating locally around Seoul, there were plenty of options for noodle soups and rice dishes. There were usually only a few sprigs of vegetables that I'd eat in these meals because I didn't like kimchi at the time. I still didn't eat red meat, chicken, or eggs, so I didn't eat much protein at all.

No doubt, you've deduced that my food choices weren't balanced while living in New York City or Seoul. I wasn't eating enough vegetables or fruit. And I wasn't eating enough protein for an active person. I was significantly lacking in all kinds of nutrients, but I wasn't aware of it. In the last chapter, I shared how you can thwart weight loss, stifle your body's metabolic processes, lose muscle, and not get the results you should be getting from food or exercise if you don't eat enough carbohydrates. The same happens if you don't eat enough protein.

About the third year into my study of nutrition, I concluded that red meat wasn't as bad as the popular media had me convinced it was. There are important vitamins and minerals in meat that are easy to get when you eat it and difficult to get if you're not eating it. Meat contains B vitamins like B12, B6, niacin, and folic acid, all of which are important in cell metabolism, brain health, and making DNA. It's a great source of iron, which carries the oxygen through your blood to your body and brain and is especially important if you're active. And it supplies zinc, which is also important for DNA as well as your immune system.

When I decided to let myself eat a lean piece of steak for dinner, I was already eating many more vegetables and fruits than I had been in my past. I was running ten-mile races and training as a triathlete, finishing two degrees simultaneously and stepping into a start-up as a founder. I had studied the physiological benefits of red meat, so I decided to try it. And I decided my first piece of red meat was going to be a high-quality piece of meat if I was going to eat it.

I remember sitting down to my first steak in a long while in that restaurant. I also remember the way I felt noticeably different the day after. In fact, I felt rejuvenated for days. I began to allow a little more meat into my diet, and to my continued surprise, I noticed that I felt more alert and was recovering from my workouts faster and with less muscle soreness. I also felt noticeably less groggy during the day. There were obviously nutrients in red meat that my body was missing.

Those are my results, and they won't be the same for everyone. Now that I know what my needs are, I rotate high-quality red meat into my meals a couple of times per week. I also make sure to vary my protein sources and eat food from the protein category with every meal. Athletic or not, active or not (although I hope you're active), we all have our own protein needs. You'll find out more about your needs in this step.

How Much Protein Do You Need for *Your* Brain and Body?

Everyone is different when it comes to protein needs. Just like carbohydrates, it's another situation where a one-size-fits-all diet just doesn't work. So, it's important to have a general idea of how much you need and have a plan to get it.

The Recommended Dietary Allowance (RDA) for both men and women (19 years and older) is 0.36 grams of protein per pound of body weight per day for baseline health. However, current research suggests that if you are over the age of 45, trying to lose weight, exercising intensely, or any combination of the three, you need more than that to prevent muscle loss. These studies show evidence that in these circumstances, we need between 0.7–1 gram of protein, per pound of body weight, per day, and possibly more. And it's not difficult to get this amount.

How much protein do *you* need? There's a calculation for you and your specific protein needs for your body weight in The Leading Edge section. Before we jump into that, there's more to know about protein than just how much to eat.

What Are Good Sources of Protein?

Animal proteins provide all the essential amino acids. That's why meats, fish, seafood, dairy, and eggs are called complete proteins. All food has some protein in it, some more than others. For example, lean animal meat offers 7–10 grams of protein per ounce. Fish and seafood will give you 4–8 grams per ounce. Eggs have about 3.5 grams per ounce. Legumes have 2–3 grams per ounce. Milk and yogurt have 1 gram per ounce. Keep in mind the more fat in the food, the less protein there will be due to displacement.

Vegetables, fruit, and even grains have protein too, but they have even less than the above. Plants offer incomplete protein. That means you need to combine a variety of plants and eat enough of them for your body to get all the amino acids. If you're a vegetarian, you need to be especially diligent about eating larger amounts of fruits, vegetables, legumes (beans), and true whole grains to get the variety of amino acids necessary to satisfy your protein needs.

Five Major Considerations About Meat Today

If you want to eat animal meat in a healthy way, there are five major considerations you'll want to keep in mind.

1. How the animal was raised: Animals that are raised on a range and cage-free are able to move more. For this reason, they'll have healthier muscle and more muscle too. Therefore, eating free-range, cage-free meat will be healthier for you as well. In addition, these animals will have less fat, and the fat they do have will be slightly higher in omega-3s, which is a healthy fat. If you're interested in supporting better treatment of animals, buying these kinds of meats will support the farmers who give animals space to live and roam. This, in turn, will encourage more of these practices.

There's misinformation going around today claiming that fat is fine to eat without restriction, but this is not the case. The consensus of most reputable scientific associations around the world is that avoiding saturated fat, which largely comes from animals, is still key to avoiding heart disease, stroke, dementia, and many kinds of cancer. We'll talk more about healthy fats in the next chapter. For now, keep in mind that less fat in your meat is healthier.

2. How the animal ate: Just like you, what an animal eats goes into its blood, muscle, and fat. If the animal meat is organic, it means the animal was fed organic food and not fed other animals or foods unnatural to their digestive system or foods covered in pesticides or grown from genetically modified organisms (GMOs), which use harmful pesticides. If the animal is fed the right way, it will be a healthier option for you, too.

3. Whether hormones and antibiotics were used: Hormones are often used in large, industrial farms (often called factory farms) to speed up the animals' growth or unnaturally increase their size. It goes without saying that if the hormones are at an unnaturally high level in the animal and you eat the animal, it's likely that those hormones will affect you too. Look for labels that say *No BGH* (bovine growth hormone).

Antibiotics are frequently given to animals living in close quarters preemptively, so they don't get sick from living in their own feces and too close to their neighbors. *Antibiotic Free* is another thing to look for when choosing animal meat. In some situations, you may not be able to know how an animal was raised or fed, or whether they were given antibiotics and hormones. If you choose meat in these cases, do the best you can to choose meats that are prepared in the healthiest way possible—which is my next point.

4. Whether the meat is processed: Processed and cured meats like bacon, salami, sausages, hot dogs, and processed deli and luncheon meats have been found to increase the risk of heart disease, type 2 diabetes, and certain kinds of cancer. In 2015, processed meat was classified by the World Health Organization as a Group 1 Carcinogen. That means there is

sufficient evidence that diets high in processed meat can cause cancer. Processed meats are defined as any meat preserved by smoking, curing, or salting or addition of chemical preservatives. It's the high amount of saturated fats, salt, and nitrites that are suspect.

That's not to say that a deli sandwich can't be eaten and enjoyed now and then. However, research today specifically suggests we keep these foods to a minimum in our diet. If you like sandwiches, look for meat that's cut off the bone. Or find meat that's uncured, without nitrates or added sodium. Eat fast-food meat, cured meat, sausages, and bacon only on special occasions.

5. How the meat is prepared: Any chef can take a very healthy, lean piece of meat and make it unhealthy. If you coat chicken in white flour and deep-fry it in oil, you can turn a 95-calorie chicken breast (with 27 calories of fat) into a breast with 280 calories (168 calories from fat). Most of the additional 200 calories and all the fat comes from the cooking oil that soaks into the breading. As you increase the fat and breading, you dilute the amount of protein per ounce, lower the nutrient density, and increase the calorie density of your food. Not to mention, you have no control over the quality of the oil used. (We'll talk about oil quality in the next chapter.) So, stay away from breaded, deep-fried meats as much as possible.

It's best to eat meat from trusted sources for quality. Generally speaking, a clean, lean cut of responsibly farmed meat will be safer to eat than meat that has been factory farmed or chopped, mixed, minced, deep-fried, or processed with other, unknown ingredients.

Step 5—Protein for How You Look, Feel, and Perform
The idea here is to make sure you're getting enough protein daily and make sure your protein is coming from healthy sources, so you continue to feel good and perform well now and long into the future.

1. Make one-quarter of each meal a serving of high-quality protein. Include protein in your snacks too, in the same proportions as below.

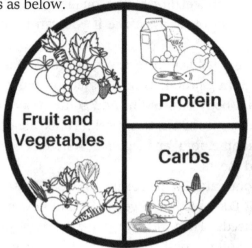

Now, each time you eat, you'll have vegetables or fruit, healthy carbs, and healthy protein. The proportions are one-half, one-quarter, and one-quarter, respectively.

It's best for you to do your own protein calculation in The Leading Edge section. However, here's a general idea of what a serving of protein is:

- Three to four ounces of lean meat, fish, or seafood. This can be estimated by the size of your flat palm.

- A cup of low-fat milk or yogurt

- A cup of legumes/ beans or food made from legumes like tofu, or bean burgers

- About three eggs

2. Choose high-quality meats. Select unprocessed, uncured meats that aren't deep-fried. And just like you've been doing with everything else, go lighter on butter, cheese, cream, sour

cream, heavy sauces, and other high-calorie, added ingredients that may be questionable for your health and can negatively affect the way you feel. Fresh, high-quality protein has a great, natural flavor all of its own. See if you can taste it without masking it.

3. Diversify. It's key for every food group. Research today shows that getting protein from a variety of sources will be the best for your body and brain. Add some new and different protein sources to meals this week. Think about fish, eggs, yogurt, edamame, tofu, and legumes. Rotate between chicken, fish, and red meats.

4. Get your data. Go to "Calculating Your Protein Needs" in The Leading Edge section to get an idea of how much protein your body needs. Then, discover what kinds of protein work best for you and the best times to eat it by journaling in your Dynamic Lifestyle Road Map.

Is Red Meat Really That Unhealthy?

There's no black-and-white, cut-and-dried answer to whether or not red meat is unhealthy. It depends on what kind of meat you're talking about, how much of it you're eating, and how it's prepared.

Recently, the nutrition science community has been discussing the fact that most research on red meat up until now has grouped all red meat into one category, without accounting for the differences between the kinds and qualities of meat. That means, when testing the health effects of red meat, there has been little distinction between meat obtained from free-range animals and meat from animals raised in poor, cramped conditions; between animals given antibiotics and hormones and those that haven't; between unprocessed and processed red meat; or even between fast-food, deep-fried meats and a lean slice of sirloin. All these sources have been grouped together when evaluating the health aspects of red meat. As you might expect, that's going to muddle the research results a bit.

Current scientific evidence points to the likelihood that the quality of the meat you eat makes a big difference in how it affects your health and longevity. Based on that, my opinion is that if you eat the healthiest types of protein and vary your protein sources throughout the week, you'll do quite well. And you'll further protect yourself by eating phytonutrients and antioxidants (fruits and vegetables) with every meal.

Often Forgotten Sources of Proteins: Legumes
Legumes are the highest protein source of all the vegetables. Legumes are beans, peas, soybeans, black beans, chickpeas, and others. You can find them dried as well as canned. Green beans are not legumes. (That's a little fact I didn't know before my nutrition education, so I thought it worth sharing.)

Lentils, kidney beans, chickpeas, and peas in particular are great sources of soluble fiber. You'll remember from the last chapter that soluble fiber, when eaten in a meal, will slow the release of blood sugar from your entire meal, helping you have more even-keeled, balanced energy for hours. It'll help you feel fuller with less food and will clean out your gut, specifically removing cholesterol and triglycerides from your system. It would be good for everyone, not only vegetarians, to get more legumes into their diet.

If you're a vegetarian, you'll want to include them in your diet regularly to ensure complete protein. If you eat legumes along with wheat, rice, or corn—and it doesn't even have to be in the same meal—you'll get all the essential amino acids.

I don't know about you, but I used to equate beans with "boring!" But it doesn't have to be so. I share a few ideas on how to add legumes to meals and keep it interesting in The Leading Edge section. If you're just beginning to eat legumes, take it slow so your digestive system can get used to the increase in fiber.

Milk and Yogurt: Fast Protein with Perks

If you can digest dairy products, you should take advantage of milk and yogurt. Just like all other animal proteins, the healthiest milk comes from farms that take good care of their cows. It's best to drink milk from a package that states it comes without rBGH (recombinant bovine growth hormone), also known as rBST (recombinant bovine somatotropin). When milk comes from a healthy source, it can be a fast, easy, and affordable way to get protein, and the calcium benefit is unbeatable.

To prevent bone loss, women need 1,000 mg of calcium per day before the age of 50 and 1,200 mg after that. Men need 1,000 mg per day before the age of 70 and 1,200 mg after that. We absorb and assimilate vitamins and minerals best from whole foods. If you take supplements, know that absorption of calcium is best when taken with food and 500 mg or less at a time. At this time, it's speculated that getting all your calcium from supplements or taking large doses at once could pose a risk to cardiovascular health. So, we need to be judicious with supplements.

A cup of low-fat milk has about 8 grams of protein (about a gram per ounce) and close to 300 mg of calcium. That's 25%–30% of your daily calcium requirement. A cup of yogurt has 9–13 grams of protein with 30%–45% of your daily calcium requirement. That's significant!

Yogurt has the additional benefit of probiotics, which keeps your gut microbiome healthy. And I was amazed to find out how well yogurt can calm a sensitive or "sour" stomach almost immediately.

Milk or yogurt can also be a fast, post-workout recovery food. These have both protein and carbs, so when you're in a pinch, they're like a fast, small meal. Since saturated fat is still associated with heart disease, go for low-fat dairy products when you can. In my opinion, a little bit of fat in these foods tastes better than fat-free—and it'll help you absorb vitamin D, which is a fat-soluble vitamin.

You may remember that I was diagnosed as lactose intolerant (which means I was unable to digest the carbohydrate in milk). I'll tell you how I got over my dairy allergy in The Leading Edge section. But I'll share here that for some, it's not the lactose that poses the problem but the kind of casein (a protein) in cow's milk that causes digestive issues. Before shunning milk completely, you might give goat or sheep milk a try, as they have the kind of casein that can be less of an irritant. I can have goat milk in my coffee and with my oatmeal, and it provides a significant amount of my daily protein and calcium intake. I try to eat yogurt several times per week for probiotics and the milk-digesting bacteria.

It's Your Choice

Choose one or two small changes to take on this week. Think outside the box and stretch a little to get healthier sources of protein.

1. If you eat out at restaurants most of the time, choose your proteins in the healthiest way possible. For example:

• Eat protein servings that match the recommended serving sizes above rather than oversized servings that take up your entire dinner plate. (Remember, we need to make room for the vegetables and other plant foods.)

• Ask how the meat is prepared if it's not clear on the menu. Avoid breaded and deep-fried meats and other kinds of preparation that reduce the nutrient density and increase the calorie density of your food.

• Cut off large areas of fat if you can and avoid meat dripping with fat and oil.

• Whenever possible, choose restaurants that advertise that their meat is free-range and antibiotic- and hormone-free.

2. Take more control and pick a couple of days this week to

make protein at home. As you might have deduced from my information about meat above, it's very hard to control the quality of meat you're eating when eating out. You usually don't know how it's been raised or fed, whether it's been treated with hormones, or how much and what kind of fat it'll have when it comes to your table. If you want to eat meat and do it in a way that prolongs your health and life, make it at home more often. While you're at it, do yourself a favor and make extra protein. Take it for lunch or heat it up for a second dinner. You'll be happy you did!

3. If you're already eating healthy proteins and making as much at home as you prefer, you can bring your nutrition up a notch with the following:

- Experiment with having a cup of beans (legumes), a bean burger, or bean soup as protein in your meal once or twice this week.

- Try eating low-fat yogurt as a protein in several snacks this week.

- Eat healthy fish a couple of times this week.

Maximize Your Opportunity for Success

Think about it: We all have a limited amount of energy per day and that includes brain energy. As leaders, we need our brainpower to be creative, to listen to people, solve problems, and make decisions. One of the best things we can do to ensure we have optimal mental capacity for the big, important, and even unexpected tasks we face as leaders is remove the need to spend mental energy on smaller decisions about basic, everyday living. Making those decisions in advance and leveraging them to support our optimal performance is the answer. Do yourself a favor this week if you haven't already and organize a routine around your healthy meals.

Your new food choices will take more mental energy until they become a habit. Having a plan to eat and a system for food isn't boring; it's smart. I'm helping you do exactly that in your Dynamic Lifestyle Road Map. We'll use all the notes you've made up until now to create your optimal food system. The goal here is that you make it easy for yourself to eat very healthy, very regularly, so you can reap all the benefits of feeling, looking, and performing optimally. Your success will come from the choices you make 90% of the time.

Acknowledge Yourself

Acknowledge yourself when you take steps toward turning your vision of a healthy and strong future into reality. Give yourself credit when you fall off the path and bounce back. It's not easy to make habit changes, but with consistency and a little planning in the beginning, your new choices will become an easy and natural part of life.

THE LEADING EDGE OF SUCCESS

These extra details will give you an edge when it comes to succeeding in each step. You can read it all or choose the topics that interest you most.

Calculating Your Protein Needs

The RDA for protein for men and women (19 years and older) is a minimum of 0.36 grams per pound of body weight per day. However, current research suggests that if you are over the age of 45, trying to lose weight, exercise intensely, or any combination of the three, you need at least 0.7–1 gram per pound. Let's do the calculation for someone who weighs 130 pounds, is over 45, and is active:

0.7g x 130 = 91g, and 1g x 130 = 130g of protein.

So, this person needs between 91–130 grams of protein every day. You can do your calculations here.

RDA/Minimum Requirement

Multiply your weight (in lbs) x .36g of protein per day.
This is your minimum requirement in grams per day.

Write Your Minimum Requirement Here:

If You're Active, over 45, or Trying to Lose Weight
Low-End Calculation

Multiply your weight (in lbs) x .7g of protein per day.
This is your low-end calculation in grams per day.

Write Your Low-End Calculation Here:

High-End Calculation

Multiply your weight (in lbs) x1g of protein per day.
This is your high-end calculation in grams per day.

Write Your High-End Calculation Here:

Believe it or not, these are conservative numbers. In a review of the current research, Examine.com found that if we're active and want to build muscle or lose fat—in other words, change our body composition—we may need upward of 1.5 grams per pound of body weight per day.

After you find your number above, divide it by the number of times you eat per day, and that's how much protein you'll want to eat in each meal and snack. You don't need to be exact; if you can get close to your range every day, you'll be doing well. Here are some numbers that'll help you understand how much protein you're getting in your food:

- Lean animal meat (beef, chicken, lamb, etc.) has 27–32 grams of protein in a serving of 3–4 ounces.
- Seafood has 18–24 grams of protein in 3–4 ounces.
- Legume beans have 15–18 grams of protein in a cup.
- A large egg has about 6 grams of protein, so 3 eggs have

18 grams of protein.

• Milk and yogurt have 8 grams of protein in a cup. Some yogurts have up to 13 grams per cup.

Nuts and Protein

Many people tell me they eat nuts for protein. Nuts are great plant foods that fit more into the healthy fat category than they do in the protein category. Nuts and seeds have about 6 grams of protein per serving, which is less than milk, yogurt, or legume beans. A serving is about a handful (about 24 almonds or 14 walnut halves), or 2 tablespoons of nut butter. No matter how you eat nuts, a serving is about 200 calories—mainly from fat. For the polyunsaturated fat benefits they offer, we should eat a serving or two of nuts daily. But I don't consider them a main source of protein.

Why We Need to Pay More Attention to Calcium

Calcium is one of the major minerals that our bones are made of. It plays an important role in muscle contraction, the contraction and dilation of our veins and arteries, nerve transmission, and hormone secretion. Our bones are essentially our body's storage place for calcium. So, any time we need more calcium, it's taken from our bones.

We lose bone mass as we get older unless we get enough calcium and vitamin D and lift weights in some manner. The combination of the three is ideal to build bones and keep them strong so they don't easily deteriorate with age. This is even more important for women, as we start to lose bone after the age of 30 if we do nothing to prevent it.

I've seen too many people who don't get enough calcium in their daily diet, especially among those who don't eat or drink milk products. Bone breakage and fractures due to osteoporosis are a serious risk for our strength and independence. And it's never too late to build more bone. I've worked with people up to the age of 80 who reversed osteopenia (the porous bone stage that precedes osteoporosis) through diet and exercise.

The additional benefit to dairy is that most of it is vitamin D-fortified. Vitamin D is also required for healthy, strong bones. Regardless of your milk tolerance, a blend of food *and* supplementation can work for you. It would be best to check your diet logs to see how much calcium you've been getting in your daily diet. Then modify your food system to get enough of it daily. The best nondairy sources of calcium are kale, bok choy, broccoli, and foods that are calcium-fortified.

Workouts and Protein

Research shows that carbs *and* protein after exercise are best. Carbs provide the fuel for rebuilding and repairing muscle and replenish glycogen stores. Protein provides the building blocks for muscle. They both induce insulin release which helps jump-start anabolism (muscle building) and stop catabolism (muscle breakdown), details of which you may remember from the last chapter. Competitive athletes are strict about eating both protein and carbs immediately after training because muscles recover faster and will produce more energy and strength for their next training session.

As a leader, the sooner you eat your first meal after intense exercise the better; you'll feel better, have less muscle soreness and pain, and be less stiff the next day. As a result, you'll be able to charge through your day with more positive energy. A small meal in the proportions we've been working on is best after a workout. If you don't have much time and can digest it, milk or yogurt is a fast alternative because they have protein and carbs.

I don't usually recommend protein drinks for three reasons: (1) most of them come packed with protein and no carbohydrate, thus providing only half of what you need; (2) real food is always better for you and provides nutrients in their most bioavailable form; and (3) it's really hard to find a protein drink that tastes good! Besides, you know the downside of drinking your food. But if you absolutely can't get enough protein from the food you're eating, a protein drink may be something to consider.

Finally, it's not only the post-workout meal that affects our recovery from intense exercise. Research shows that it's more effective to continue eating enough protein throughout the day than to rely on a giant dose of protein right after your workout. Our muscles will rebuild for at least a day and sometimes more, and we need to provide them with the nutrition they need to do that.

Tryptophan and Carbs for Sleep

As you might remember, the amino acid tryptophan helps make serotonin, the hormone that helps you relax. Eating tryptophan in the evening has been associated with slightly longer sleep duration and better sleep.

You may remember from the last chapter that carbohydrates help you relax as well. Carbs also help to absorb tryptophan, so in this equation, one plus one is greater than two! You might have heard that turkey has tryptophan, but it's in many other foods. You'll find it highest in foods like eggs, soy, seeds, fish, animal meat, and dairy products. You don't need to focus on getting a specific kind of protein at night, along with your carbs. This is just another example of how all the food groups work synergistically for your benefit both day and night.

How I Became Lactose Tolerant Again

Probiotics are microorganisms that reach the intestine in an active state. Probiotics have been found to eliminate or reduce food allergies, improve your ability to digest food, and reduce GI distress. This is because the healthy, live bacteria actually stay inside your gut, live there, and ultimately help you digest food. The bacteria in yogurt is the kind that digests milk and breaks it down so it turns into yogurt. These bacteria can ultimately help you digest milk too.

I was in my twenties—prime bone-building age—when I was diagnosed as lactose intolerant. I stopped eating all milk products and started supplementing with probiotics and calcium pills. I tried extremely hard to get enough calcium without eating dairy. I had no idea that it takes 28 cups of broccoli to get the same amount of calcium as a cup of milk. I ate a lot of broccoli but not enough!

After studying probiotics in my coursework, I tried yogurt to combat some recurring digestive problems I was having, completely unassociated with the lactose intolerance. I learned that the bacteria in yogurt could donate healthy bacteria to my gut microbiome and help my immune system. Once I started eating yogurt, lo and behold, my digestive ills went away. And if I ate a small amount of yogurt regularly, like half a cup, three to four times per week, they stayed away.

After eating yogurt for a couple of years, I realized I was able to eat and drink small portions of milk products without any help from digestive pills. Today I can drink a small milk latte at the local coffee shop but not more than one per day. I can eat real cheese on top of my homemade pizzas. I have tolerance for about a cup of goat milk daily if I want it. And I can eat ice cream in small doses. According to current research on the gut microbiome, it's highly probable the reason for this is because my digestive system incorporated the milk-digesting bacteria from the yogurt and now it helps *me* digest milk. Pretty fascinating, I think!

To ensure your yogurt has probiotics that work, make sure it says "live and active cultures" in the ingredients. If you're going to try this, start with a very small amount of yogurt, like a tablespoon or two, a couple of days per week and slowly increase the amount from there.

Creative Ways to Eat Yogurt

You can add some extra protein and calcium to your day by eating yogurt, and it goes with many types of foods—sweet or savory.

- Low-fat yogurt is a great snack. Try vanilla for less sugar. Eat it with real fruit or a little granola. Believe it or not, a tablespoon of honey or jam in plain yogurt will be much less added sugar than if you bought it presweetened.
- Plain, low-fat Greek yogurt is a great substitute for sour cream. It tastes great on top of baked potatoes, salads, soups, chili, fish, dumplings, even a sandwich or wrap. Try some on top of roasted cauliflower or Brussels sprouts or in your cauliflower mash.
- Use low-fat plain Greek yogurt for dipping vegetables. It's fine by itself, or you can mix in a few herbs and spices, like dill, fennel, onion, garlic, pepper, turmeric, or cayenne.
- Goat and sheep yogurt have additional probiotic cultures that are different from cows-milk yogurt. Give them a try for variety; they might be easier for you to digest if cow milk doesn't agree with you. If nothing else, they'll add additional, healthy bacteria to your gut.
- Drinking kefir or ayran are two additional ways to get probiotics and milk-digesting bacteria.

Easy Ways to Eat Legumes

- Beans in soup (lentil, minestrone, or other)
- Beans on salad
- Bean chili (meat or meatless)
- Beans in pasta sauce or on pasta
- A veggie burger made with beans or peas

What About Hummus?

Hummus is made out of legumes, specifically chickpeas. But it's 50–70 calories for 2 tablespoons, with calories mostly from olive oil. Because of its high-calorie content, we're going to call it a healthier kind of condiment. Eat hummus like you'd eat mayonnaise, butter, or any other creamy spread or dip—a couple of tablespoons per serving does the trick. Or, if you like chickpeas, you can add them to your soup or salad.

Five-Star Restaurant Secrets

1. Just like everything else, when it comes to protein, fresh tastes best! As a bonus, fresh protein that comes from healthy sources will also last a day or two longer in the refrigerator.

2. If you freeze meat, make sure to vacuum-pack it, so ice doesn't get into the muscle and break down the protein. It changes the texture and flavor.

3. When it comes to cooking meat, use a cooking thermometer. It's better than slicing meat and losing all the juice before it's done. While meat is being cooked, most of the juices will flow to the center. Once it comes out of the oven or stove and starts to cool, the juices will flow back out to the edges. That's why, after cooking, we want to give meat a rest period of about 10 minutes for the juices to redistribute. If you use a thermometer to gauge whether the meat is done, you lose less juice while cooking, and your meat will be juicier and softer when you eat it.

4. If you're using canned beans, rinse them before eating. This removes up to 40% of the salt. It also removes the gel that forms on the beans.

5. If you cook dried beans, soak them in water overnight and then throw out the water. An even faster trick is to place them in boiling water with the top off for 5 minutes and discard the water. This helps excess nitrogen escape and takes away the dreaded gas effect.

Envisioning Your Success

You only need to spend a few seconds making the right food choices, but the effects of your choices will compound over time. Whenever you feel low on willpower or mental energy to choose the best foods, call to mind your vision of yourself as a leader with a strong and capable body and mind now and far into the future. Choosing the healthiest proteins and including some in each meal will help you make that future a reality.

Your food will support you in being mentally and physically strong and resilient. Setting up a system for that now is well worth the effort. When you create a system to make healthy choices, your choices will eventually become habit and take less energy to make. Head over to the Dietary Lifestyle Road Map where we'll put the finishing touches on your system.

We're almost complete. But first, we need to talk about the kind of conversations exceptional leaders have with others. And we need to discuss the big fat fads!

| CHAPTER 6 |
LEADERSHIP CONVERSATIONS AND THE BIG FAT FADS

This is a case where one plus one is greater than two. All of these steps are synergistic, and the benefits of your efforts will compound over time. Keep eating what you now know is right for the health of your body and brain and will benefit your leadership capacity. It'll all come together nicely as you get the hang of it.

See yourself as being successful in this. Be open to the fact that your new eating habits may create even more profound and positive results than you imagined. In the last chapter, we discussed future visioning. Now I'd like to discuss turning your vision into conversations that inspire transformation in others.

Leadership Conversations

Leadership almost always involves helping people through change or transformation. In *The Three Laws of Performance,* Steve Zaffron and Dave Logan explain how leaders inspire people to change by helping them "envision a future they may not currently see."

To be inspiring, leaders have distinctly different kinds of conversations. First of all, they invite people they lead to participate in creating a shared vision of the future. Rather than simply following someone else's vision, which is minimally motivating, participants can see themselves in a new future that they helped create. This is how a leader empowers and enlists people in making changes. This is how a leader excites people and stimulates the kind of change that can take on a life of its own, even without a leader's presence.

Second, inspiring leaders avoid conversations that are unproductive, negative, or focused on the past. Instead, they stay focused on forward-looking, productive conversations. I'm not saying that a leader is someone who pretends that everything's always great or ignores reality. Rather, keeping conversations keenly focused on problem-solving, future planning, and moving ahead is how leaders lead with hope and inspiration, lifting everyone's energy up in the process.

It's important to be your own inspiration when leading yourself through change. Pay attention to the conversations you have in your mind. When you notice yourself speaking in ways that are unproductive, negative, or coming from the past, stop and redirect your self-talk into something that's forward-thinking, positive, and productive. The conversations you have in your mind now about how you will take care of yourself uncompromisingly need to be as powerful and positive as the conversations you have with the people you lead.

Eating the right fuel is important to your effectiveness as a leader. Throw away any conversation about how it's difficult to eat the right foods or how it *can't* be done. Dismiss any conversation about how you don't know how to eat. You don't need to jump onto any new diet that comes out. It doesn't help or serve you. Your conversation now is that you know how to eat right and you *do* it! You use food as your tool for strength, energy, clarity, stamina, and optimal performance, and you're getting better at it every day.

Once finished with this book and the exercises, you can feel confident in your knowledge about how food works in your body. You'll have a strong foundation of food habits that will support you in all things you do as a leader and elsewhere. Continue to lead yourself forward and onward. Continue to be inspirational, for yourself as well as others.

What and Why

Diets and fads can feel inspiring at first. They'll promise an ideal life, free of physical ailments and easy, fast weight loss. But they can quickly lose their luster once the day-to-day routine sets in—broad dietary restrictions and strict rules can weigh heavy on a leadership lifestyle that requires agility and flexibility. Besides that, you can't afford to waste time and energy changing your diet and following specific food formulas if it doesn't ultimately serve your greatest physical and mental potential for the long run.

Today, the macronutrient in the spotlight is fat; high-fat diets abound, disseminating misinformation galore. I'll discuss some of these next. In doing so, I'll help you get on track to eating the kinds of fats that are good for your body and your brain and keep you feeling light and energized after a meal. I'll help you steer away from the kinds of fats that are known to be associated with illness and diseases like heart disease, Alzheimer's, and dementia that can take you out of the leadership game altogether. We'll also take a look at how much fat is really needed for your body and brain to be a productive leader and how that differs from what the fads are telling you.

What Is Fat?

Fat is an important macronutrient. As you learned in chapter 2, macronutrients are the nutrients we need to eat the most of to sustain the health and vitality of our body and mind. They are the nutrients that provide us with calories.

Fat, like carbs, is also a chain of carbon, hydrogen, and oxygen atoms, except with a more complex structure. And like carbs, the body also takes these large chains apart and turns them into glucose but with a side of fatty acids. Fat is a long-burning fuel, and the body is constantly breaking it down along with carbohydrates to ensure our fuel needs are covered.

Along with providing us with energy in the form of calories, here's why fat is important:

• Our cell membranes are largely made up of fat.

• Our nerves also have a fatty outer covering called the myelin sheath. This includes the network of nerves that make up our brain.

• When we eat fat, it helps us absorb fat-soluble vitamins: vitamins A, D, E, and K.

• It protects and cushions our organs and joints.

• It helps our skin stay soft and young-looking.

• When we eat fat in conjunction with other healthy nutrients in the right amounts, it helps us feel full and satisfied, maintain our stamina, and keeps us fueled for getting things done.

Looking at the Major Fads of Today

There's much controversy in America today regarding which diet is better: the high-fat diet or the high-carb diet. As you know by now, I don't advocate any diet, only healthy, well-rounded choices. And the conversations around high-fat fads have caused many people to question what "healthy eating" really is.

High-fat diets include some of the Paleo-type diets that suggest 50% or more of your calories come from fat to the ketogenic diets which suggest anywhere from 75%–90% of your calories come from fat.

On the other hand, diets that recommend 50%–60% carbs include the DASH diet, the MIND diet, the Mediterranean diet, and all vegetarian and vegan diets. These are eating plans high in vegetables and plant foods that have proven over and over again to outperform all others when it comes to preventing and fighting countless diseases, keep us living longer, and maintaining our abilities to perform at our best, both physically and mentally.

So, why is there a controversy? Many supporters of the

high-fat fads argue that we've been prescribing high-carb diets for the last 50 years, and yet the American population is obese and diabetic and only getting worse. For that reason, we need to do something drastically different.

They argue that the diet that nutritionists, nutrition-scientists, and government agencies have been recommending isn't working. Therefore, we should do the exact opposite and, instead of eating 50% or more of our calories from carbohydrates, we should eat 50%–90% of our calories from fat. You can read details about "How Fat Went from Bad Guy to Miracle Nutrient" in The Leading Edge section. If you've been following along up to now, you may already know the logical responses to those arguments, but I'll sum it up for you here.

While it's true that the majority of nutrition science professionals still recommend that most of the calories in your diet come from carbohydrates, you already know that carbohydrates are not only sugar, pizza, white bread, pretzels, doughnuts, French fries, and potato chips—even though they're the kind of carbs Americans eat most. (But not you, at least not anymore!) Carbs include all the healthy, fiber-filled, nutrient-filled, antioxidant-filled plant foods. These include both watery and carb-dense vegetables, fruit, real whole grains, and legumes. As you already know, the specific recommendation is that *these* fibrous, nutrient-dense foods make up the majority of the carbohydrates in your diet, and the majority of the food you eat.

In fact, the American population hasn't been eating according to the USDA guidelines by a longshot. If we were doing so and still trending toward higher levels of obesity, diabetes, and heart disease, it would certainly give us reason to change our tune. But when the last Dietary Guidelines committee met, they concluded the following:

1. The U.S. population, on the whole, does not meet recommendations for vegetables, fruit, dairy, or whole

grains and hasn't done so for many years.

2. We eat too much salt and saturated fat, refined grains, and added sugar.

3. We don't get enough vitamin A, vitamin D, vitamin E, vitamin C, folate, iron, calcium, magnesium, fiber, and potassium. (Most are nutrients obtained from carbohydrate-rich plant food.)

To be fair, fat was named the nutrient "bad guy" for years. Many "fat-phobics" came out of the low-fat diet trends. I used to be one! And still, at this point, you know that no single nutrient is good or bad. We need to have all nutrients in our diet to function optimally. Yet there are definitely good and bad food choices, and we'll be discussing good and bad *fat choices* in this chapter.

Research-Supported Fat Facts

I'll explain these in more detail going forward. For now, here's a summary of what the current research supports:

1. Trans fats are the worst for heart disease and the unhealthiest of all fats.

2. Saturated fat is still strongly associated with heart disease and dementia.

3. Cholesterol doesn't need to be avoided like we thought it did.

4. Monounsaturated and polyunsaturated fats are healthy for our body and brain, although, we need only a little bit each day.

5. Omega-3 and omega-6 are types of polyunsaturated fat. Our brain and body need them, but we can't make them, which is why we call them essential fats. But we only need a little each day to satisfy our requirement.

6. Fat calories still count. Gram per gram, they have over twice as many calories as protein and carbohydrates.

7. Fat is out of the "bad-guy" category, but, as you gathered

from the last chapter, we don't want to go "whole hog" on eating bacon. In short:

• Some of the right kinds of fat = good

• Lots of all kinds of fat = not good

That's what you'll be focusing on next—getting the right amounts and the right kinds of fat.

Brain Fat into Fiction

There are many unfounded leaps from fat fact to fiction being made by fad diets today. One of which is that our brains are made of fat; therefore, we need to eat more fat of all kinds to keep our brains healthy. But another nutrient is even more prominent in the brain, which I'll cover shortly.

Dr. Mosconi, author of *Brain Food*, says, "Saturated fat is not on the brain's grocery list." While it's true that all our nerves including the nerves in our brain have an outer covering of fat and cholesterol, the brain only needs to absorb saturated fat up until adolescence. After that, most forms of saturated fat can't even get inside the brain. When our brain does need fat, it needs the kind we can't make on our own. More specifically, it needs the "essential fatty acids."

You already know that your brain's preferred fuel for thinking is glucose. Your brain will use ketones for fuel in emergency situations, like starvation. (Ketones are a product of fat-breakdown when there's not enough glucose available.) But, since ketones aren't the brain's preferred source of fuel, they aren't the most efficient source of energy for your brain either.

Recall that your brain burns 20% of your calories, and it requires consistent energy to work optimally. So, it's best to have your blood glucose running at normal levels all day by eating regularly and eating long-burning types of fuel in the form of complex carbs from vegetables, fruits, and whole grains. It's quite convenient that these healthy foods not only provide our brains with energy, but research finds these are the foods which also reduce the rate of brain cell aging and death and lower our risk of stroke and dementia. There's research showing diets high in vegetables, fruit, whole grains, and fish, accompanied by lean, high-quality proteins that I've mentioned, are associated with larger brain volumes—especially gray matter—which translates to better thinking and remembering. These are also the diets that are linked to slowing, and even reversing, the aging of our DNA.

On the other hand, there's evidence that those with diets highest in saturated fat double their risk of developing Alzheimer's disease. These diets are also implicated in causing a weak gut microbiome, leading to digestive problems, inflammation, and a compromised immune system. Current research recognizes that our gut microbiome influences our brain and nervous system. Studies suggest disturbances in our gut microbiome may be linked to autoimmune and metabolic disorders, autism, depression, anxiety, and neurological disorders like Parkinson's. There are many brain-related reasons to keep our gut microbiome healthy. That being said, the specific recommendation by nutrition scientists and the nutrition community at large is *not to add more fat* of all kinds to our diet but to *eat healthy fats* and less saturated fat. More specifically, we need to focus on eating the essential fatty acids. And we don't need much of them to do the trick.

Water, Not Fat

Water makes up about 80% of the living human brain. In the research we have to date, it's been found that even mild dehydration can reduce your ability to think with speed and accuracy, reduce your attention span and alertness, cause headaches and brain fog, and affect your mood. Long-term dehydration, over time, can cause parts of the brain to get thinner and lose volume. Our individual needs for water depend on our environment and activity levels, but current research finds about 8 to 13 cups of water per day, for women and men respectively, is a good rule of thumb.

As we explored in chapter 3, when we're getting the nutrition we need in the morning after an eight or more hour overnight fast, our brain works better. Water is a nutrient too, and we'll have been without it overnight as well. It doesn't give you the same jolt as caffeine does, but when you hydrate your brain first thing in the morning, you can observe an uptick in alertness. Staying hydrated throughout the day can markedly improve your performance and keep you from feeling unnecessarily tired. When I put water into my morning system and started drinking it first thing, I was amazed at how much more alert I felt, even before my first sip of coffee. Often, if I've eaten and had enough sleep but am still tired in the afternoon, I find it's because I haven't had enough water that day. I can feel awake and alert again after just one glass. You'll probably find like I did that you need less caffeine throughout the day when you're well-hydrated. If you've already implemented the changes I've suggested so far, drinking enough water will put the final nail in the coffin of your afternoon slumps.

Fat and Body Fat

As I've said before, calories still count! If you want to feel your best, have an abundance of energy, and reduce your risk for many of the prevalent illnesses in the country today, maintaining low body fat has proven to help a lot. If we eat too many calories from any food, we feel slower after meals and, in the long run, gain body fat. It's easier to eat more calories from fat because:

- Fat has 9 calories per gram

- Carbs have 4 calories per gram

- Protein has 4 calories per gram

Extra calories from fat, just like any food, goes into our fat cells to be stored for later. Additionally, fat has no fiber or water to help us feel full. And since we can consume more calories in less volume with fat, we can eat more calories than we need and hardly notice like Jon in did in Step 1.

Then why do people say their fat practically melts away when they go on a high-fat diet? Because people on these diets ultimately end up eating fewer calories. One of the best and most thorough studies to date comparing low-fat and low-carbohydrate diets—a study out of Stanford University in early 2018—showed that study participants on both the healthy high-fat and the healthy high-carb diet ended up eating fewer calories. Both groups lost the same amount of weight on average. Both groups reduced body fat, waist circumference, and blood pressure. However, those on the low-carb, high-fat diet ended up with higher LDL cholesterol (known as the "bad" cholesterol). They also ate less fiber, the very ingredient that fights blood sugar spikes, supports a healthy gut microbiome, and combats high cholesterol in the first place.

Fat as Fuel
Fat promotes cholecystokinin (also known as CCK), which is a hormone that helps you feel satisfied during your meal and for a couple of hours afterward. It's not common knowledge, but protein also promotes the release of CCK. Fat doesn't offer the same gut-full or belly-full feeling that we get when we eat fiber-filled foods. It also doesn't slow down our digestion or regulate our blood sugar as fiber-filled foods do. But, as you know, it's good to have both short- and long-term staying power from our meals. So, a small amount of the healthier kinds of fat, along with protein and complex carbs, will take you a long way.

Because fat is a calorie-dense fuel, it can be useful when you need to carry more calories in smaller packages. For example, it's the reason why the Sherpas in the Himalayas drink the equivalent of butter in their tea—they need lots of calories to climb those challenging mountains every day. And carrying big bags of food on their backs wouldn't be very efficient. One of the more popular fads of today—drinking butter or oil in coffee—was born out of this Sherpa tradition.

But, in our culture right now, we're not climbing mountains every day. Add to that, as we get on in age, we tend to spend more time in the seated position, which means we spend less energy overall. For many of us, moving up in our career means taking on more administrative work and sitting down more. Another hit to our metabolism comes with the natural loss of muscle as we age. So, if we do nothing about it, as we go through life, we need to eat fewer and fewer calories to avoid gaining body fat and losing muscle. For a leader, this is not the ideal physical state to be in when it comes to keeping long hours full of energy, strength, and stamina.

But this fate doesn't have to be yours. You can do something about it. As I've mentioned previously, you can maintain your muscle mass and keep a high metabolism with exercise, even as you get older. We can increase our metabolism even further by taking daily walks, along with standing up and moving every hour. For a leader, that's great news, because it means you can get two things done at once by getting up from your desk regularly: (1) strengthen your body and mind, and (2) strengthen your relationships with those you're leading. After all, one of the best things you can do as a leader is to be physically present, participating with, listening to, and observing your team. Whether you have a team to visit or not, set a timer on your computer or phone for an hour and get up and move.

In addition to movement that increases metabolism, eating regularly is key to maintaining your metabolism. If your body thinks it's starving, your metabolism will be downregulated. That's why it's important to be able to eat more food without overeating calories, which you now know how to do.

You already know that fiber, carbohydrate, and protein work together to provide satisfaction and sustainable energy from your meals. Eating the right kind of fat is the final piece of the puzzle when it comes to creating meals that support your optimal performance.

Brenda's Story

Brenda was looking in the full-length mirror one morning before another big presentation at work. She was wearing one of her favorite presentation power-outfits: a navy-blue skirt-suit with a white ruffled blouse. She used to feel so good in it. But now, there were lumps and it pulled in places. This time around it wasn't helping her feel powerful, and it wasn't going to add to her persuasive value. She pursed her lips together and went into her closet for one of her "everyday" suits instead.

I mentioned Brenda briefly in Chapter 1. She was a cancer survivor who had been in remission for 10 years and ate what most would consider an extremely clean diet. She was a decision-maker in a government agency in D.C. and led a very active life as a competitive endurance athlete. Even though she was athletic, she had been holding on to weight around her waist, and she couldn't figure out how to get rid of it. She knew that abdominal fat is the most dangerous fat to have, linked to many metabolic problems, and she didn't want to put herself into any further danger. With cancer 10 years behind her, she asked me to help her optimize her diet to improve her health, as well as how she looked and felt.

As we talked at our first meeting, she was completely honest with me. Of course, she wanted to do everything she could for her health. But she admitted her physique was dragging her down. Her belly was making her look 15 years older. She didn't feel like her usual, stellar self when standing in front of people, and she missed wearing some of her favorite clothes that she had spent time and energy collecting. On top of that, she had a new boyfriend and summer was coming. She wanted to feel attractive and carefree when she went on dates in the hot and humid D.C. weather.

After she journaled for about 10 days, we had our first

meeting to review her data together. I saw that she didn't eat processed foods or any kind of junk. To many people, her diet would have looked perfect. But there were two things that stood out to me: her snacks and her go-to dinners in particular were causing her calorie count to go above her needs. The food she was eating certainly looked clean and healthy, but I suspected some health halo foods in the fat category were probably the reason she was holding extra weight around her middle.

Most days of the week, Brenda was skipping lunch and eating a cup or more of trail mix with nuts and dried fruit to get her through her afternoon slump. Nuts are a great source of healthy fats, but they pack a lot of calories into a small package. They can easily contribute far more than your daily energy needs if you don't pay attention to how much you're eating. A cup of nuts alone is 800 calories. And although dried fruit has fiber and vitamins, you'll get many more calories from concentrated sugar in a handful of dried fruit than if you just ate the whole fruit. On some days, Brenda was eating a thousand or more calories of trail mix on top of her regular meals.

Brenda was eating lots of vegetables for their cancer-fighting properties, which was super. One of her systems for eating healthy was to make a huge pot of one of her favorite Indian dishes on the weekends. She'd then have it for several nights' dinner in the late evenings when she got home. These recipes were full of great vegetables and spices known for their antioxidants. However, they also had saturated fat from coconut milk, coconut oil, and ghee (a clarified butter). She'd heard from various sources that these ingredients were healthy now, so she used them liberally. She let me know, though, that there were nights when she'd go to bed feeling heavy and then she wouldn't sleep well. She knew she'd eaten too much food, but sometimes, she was so hungry when she got home that she'd eat really fast and end up unintentionally overeating.

These two food habits were pushing Brenda too far above her calorie needs on a regular basis, even though she was athletic. She was also not eating regularly during the day, and she was overeating at night. This, along with her desk job, was causing fat to accumulate around her middle.

When we talked about the trail mix, she said half-jokingly, "I thought it was what fit people eat!" I explained that it can be what fit people eat, because it's easy to carry more calories in smaller packages on long bike rides or hikes. It can also be what fit people eat if they can't eat enough calories to sustain their body weight with the amount of exercise they're doing. But this isn't the case for most people, especially if we sit at a desk for most of the workday. There are better ways to snack, even if you exercise.

As for the dinner, we got together a couple of times for some food prep. We experimented with using much less of the saturated fat—coconut oil, coconut milk, and butter—and added more vegetables to increase the juice and flavor. We parceled out the meals into containers so she could heat and eat one serving easily in the late evenings.

Instead of trail mix, she started snacking on fresh fruit and a single handful of nuts. Sometimes she'd bring to work fresh vegetables with plain Greek yogurt as dip. On some days, she'd simply bring extra lunch and save it for later. She established that her favorite recovery snack to have in the car after her late-night workouts was nut butter on whole-grain crackers with a side of sliced apple.

We worked on her life-balance, too. We got her to a place where she felt comfortable with taking 40 minutes to herself for lunch. This enabled her to move more as she'd walk to and from the cafeteria. While there, she might buy food or eat a meal from home. She later told me that she was grateful for this time in the middle of the day to think and breathe. I also helped her get more efficient workouts in the gym, so she could get more results from the time that she invested there.

Brenda lost the weight around her middle that she'd been fighting for years. With the system that we devised, she was fueling herself on a regular schedule and eating more nutrient-dense foods. She was also getting better sleep because she was eating less heavy food at night. This, plus time to herself during lunch, helped her have more stamina for leadership which included marathons of meetings and decision-making.

I met with her about a year after our work together for coffee. She was thrilled with her results. Not only did she take the weight off her middle, she also took years off her face; she looked younger than her age. "I went to a college reunion and someone asked what kind of work I had done," she said as she laughed. "Best thing ever, though," she said, "is now I can wear my favorite clothes!"

A Deeper Dive

Before discussing your final step, we need to dive a little deeper into the details of fats. For more information on where to find these fats in food, see The Leading Edge section "Where to Find Fats."

Recall that the four different types are:

- Trans fats

- Saturated fat

- Monounsaturated fats

- Polyunsaturated fats

Trans fats are strongly associated with elevating risk for heart disease and stroke and increasing whole-body inflammation. These are found in hydrogenated oils, processed foods and deep-fried foods.

Current scientific evidence still supports that saturated fats are linked to cardiovascular disease. It's been said by neuroscientists, and I predict you'll hear it more often, "What's good for the heart is good for the brain." A number of studies have shown that those who eat the most saturated fat have a higher rate of cognitive decline, dementia with age, and Alzheimer's. Saturated fat is mainly found in animal fat and only three types of plant oils: coconut, palm, and palm kernel oils.

Monounsaturated and polyunsaturated fats are good for the heart and the brain. They help reduce LDL cholesterol levels in your blood, which can lower your risk of heart disease and stroke. They're an integral part of your cell membranes. Oils rich in these fats also contribute vitamin E to the diet, an antioxidant that's good for the brain and body. These oils are obtained from nuts, seeds, olives, and avocados.

Omega-6 and omega-3 fatty acids are polyunsaturated fats and they're the essential fatty acids, so we need to eat them regularly. But we only need them in small amounts, and they come from different sources.

Omega-3 is involved in hormone production and optimal brain and nerve function. DHA, a long form of omega-3, is particularly abundant in the cerebral cortex of the brain. There are studies that show having sufficient amounts of omega-3 in your diet can lower your risk of cognitive decline, even reduce your risk of Alzheimer's. The American Heart Association says that omega-3 can decrease the risk of arrhythmias (abnormal heartbeats), which can lead to sudden death, decrease triglyceride levels, slow the growth rate of atherosclerotic plaque, and help lower blood pressure. It may also reduce inflammation and curb stiffness and joint pain from arthritis.

Current knowledge is that omega-6 and omega-3 compete for the same receptors in our brain. We need a ratio of 4:1 omega-6 to omega-3 (some neuroscientists say 2:1). But Americans are getting an overabundance of omega-6, which is found in most plant oils, and not enough omega-3. It's a double-whammy since too much omega-6 can block our ability to absorb omega-3. The best remedy for this is to purposefully eat omega-3 weekly.

The best way to get omega-3 is from natural sources. Supplements are unregulated and don't always have what they claim to have in them. And we absorb and assimilate our nutrients best from natural food sources. The dietary guidelines are to eat at least two servings (approximately 8 ounces) of fatty fish per week to get enough omega-3. You'll be working on getting the omegas, as well as monounsaturated and polyunsaturated fats, in this step.

Step 6—Avoiding the Big Fat Fads

The current recommendation by the U.S. and many other countries' health agencies is that 20%–30% of your total calories come from healthy fats and no more than 10% of your total calories come from saturated fat. The easiest way to make sure you get the right amounts of the right kinds of fat is to have a little of the right kind with each meal. Here's how you can do it with ease:

1. Get monounsaturated and polyunsaturated fats by including a small portion of either nuts, seeds, olives, avocado, or oils from these plants in each meal.

• A serving of oil is a tablespoon. You can estimate that as the size of your whole thumb.

• A serving of nuts is a quarter of a cup. You can estimate that by covering the surface of the palm of your hand.

• A serving of avocado is about half of a medium avocado.

If you're interested: Oil has 120 calories per tablespoon, nuts have 200 calories per quarter cup, and half of a medium avocado has about 150 calories.

2. Get your omega-3 fat. If you haven't started eating two servings of fish as of last week, it's time to start this week. Aim to eat two or three servings of omega-3-rich fish as an alternative to meat for your brain and nerve health. A serving of fish is 3 to 4 ounces. Make it baked, steamed, or grilled, not deep-fried.

3. Continue to steer away from processed food as much as possible. These are the foods that can sneak in the trans fats. Read the labels on packaged foods and stay away from hydrogenated oils and partially hydrogenated oils, which is where trans fats hide.

4. Saturated fat comes mainly from animals. Eat less fat from animals by choosing lean meats and keeping foods like bacon and butter to a minimum.

5. When you eat cheese, keep it down to a serving or two, a couple of times per week. A serving of cheese is 1.5 ounces; that's about the size of your index and middle finger. It has good qualities like calcium, protein, and enzymes, but it's also mainly saturated fat.

When you eat cheese, make sure it's real! Try to stay away from what I call "fake cheese" labeled as "cheese food," "cheese product," or "cheese spread" made with additives like oil, salts, and colors. Fake cheese can be found in restaurants that want to cut costs and in your grocery store. Real cheese will have only a few ingredients that you recognize: milk, salt, and sometimes rennet, cultures, or enzymes. The taste is milky and not oily.

6. Watch the labels for coconut oil, palm oil, and palm kernel oils. Try to eat these in low quantities, too. (More on coconut oil coming up.)

7. Drink more water every day.

Although there are seven points here, most of these are habits you've already been working on. Keep all the rest going!

Here's what your meal portions will look like now:

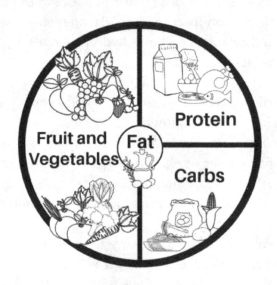

My Clients Were Going Cuckoo for Coconut Oil

I was in a video conference with a group from one of my online courses. A student who desperately wanted to lose weight was putting coconut oil on his toast instead of butter every day, because he thought it would help him lose weight and fight Alzheimer's disease, too. That didn't sound right to me, but I stayed quiet for the time being.

Afterward, another student spoke up. She was experimenting with coconut oil in coffee. She said if she only drank that in the morning, she'd have energy right up until lunch. Based on the messages she was getting from popular media, she felt strongly that it was helping her metabolize better. As an aside, she was also starting to have some gastric distress.

Neither of these sounded like healthy dietary changes to me, but the coconut oil information had just started coming out. I let them all know that I'd get back to them about my conclusion on the coconut oil and saved my comments until I investigated further.

By the time the high-fat fads started becoming popular

again, I had already finished my study in nutrition and had been working with clients in nutrition for some years. With my solid understanding of nutrition, I was pretty immune to the fads. Not to mention, I don't read diet books. And I don't read third-party nutrition information unless it's written by someone I've vetted and trust.

I looked into the research that was cited by the extreme coconut oil claims. I found (surprise, surprise) that the research was being misunderstood at the very least. At worst, it was being misused. As it turns out, the coconut oil fad started with the research of Marie-Pierre St-Onge, PhD. Her study found that the saturated fat in coconut oil, also known as MCT (medium chain triglyceride), had the potential to increase metabolism and boost weight loss. The first problem with this was that she used a special 100% MCT oil in her research, and natural coconut oil has 13%–14% MCT.

People would need to eat 10 tablespoons of coconut oil per day to get the same amount of MCT that St-Onge used. But that wasn't mentioned in the hype that pop media was feeding people. Coconut oil has the same number of calories as other oils (120 calories per tablespoon). If you eat 10 tablespoons, you'll be eating 1,200 calories per day of coconut oil! For some, that's an entire day's worth of calories. You can forget about eating any other foods with known, brain-boosting, body-fortifying nutrients. To say nothing of the bowling ball feeling you'd have in your stomach which can really put a damper on your energy.

Coconut oil is about 82% saturated fat. That's higher levels of saturated fat than butter. One tablespoon adds up to more than 11 grams of saturated fat, nearly the total daily limit of 13 grams recommended by the American Heart Association. At this time, it seems that MCT oil may not have the negative effect on heart disease that other saturated fats do. But studies have found that doses lower than that which St. Onge used don't increase calorie burn, increase metabolism, or improve cardiovascular disease risk factors. Despite that, MCT oil is still being proclaimed to be a miracle ingredient. As you now know, there are no miracle ingredients, and all food works together in complex ways.

There's a YouTube video that went viral, where a wife claims to have fed her husband coconut oil and his Alzheimer's regressed. I get asked frequently: Does that mean that we should eat coconut oil or MCT oil to prevent Alzheimer's? Not exactly. In Alzheimer's, the brain loses its ability to use glucose, but it may still be able to use ketones. While it could be a way to feed a brain with Alzheimer's (and I'm not an expert on that, so I can't speak to that point), it's not the recommended way to feed a healthy brain.

So, is coconut oil anything special? No. It's another oil to have at your disposal for cooking, and it will add a slightly coconutty taste to the food. It's got a higher "smoke point" than olive oil, which means it can fry things at higher temperatures than olive oil before it starts smoking on the stove. It's not going to solve all health problems or help you lose weight faster. The general recommendation by nutrition scientists is to limit your intake.

It's Your Choice

If you regularly eat foods that are higher in saturated fat, start to taper down a little. Here are some ways to do it. Stretch a little with this, and make sure you're having positive and forward-moving conversations about changing your food choices.

1. Take control. If you mainly eat at restaurants, here are some ways to be more in control of what you get:

• Eat deep-fried and breaded food less often. Instead, opt for baked, broiled, steamed, or roasted foods. This was part of your last step, so just continue it here.

• Ask your waiter questions like how much cheese, butter,

and/or oil comes on the dish. If it sounds like too much, ask for the chef to "go light" on the cheese/butter/oil.

• Ask for toppings and dressings on the side, and you'll avoid hundreds of unnecessary calories and hidden, questionable saturated fat and oils.

• Look around at other customers' plates as you enter a restaurant to get an idea of how the chefs are cooking the food. If it looks like a dish is drowning in oil or butter, don't order it.

2. Take it down a notch. When you prepare food at home, it's much easier to make sure the fat you eat is high quality. And high quality always translates into high flavor. When it comes to full-fat dairy like cheese, butter, cream, and ice cream, a little goes a long way. Experiment with using less fat; see more on that in The Leading Edge section.

3. Downsize dessert. Share your full-fat dessert with friends and cut a large dessert into small pieces immediately when it comes to the table.

Acknowledge Yourself
Acknowledge yourself when you make choices that are better than those you've been making in the past, especially when it's difficult. Like sugar and salt, some fat can make food enjoyable. You don't have to give it all up. But think outside the box and get creative to eat more of the best kinds of fat for your brain and body and less of the rest.

THE LEADING EDGE OF SUCCESS

These extra details will give you an edge when it comes to succeeding in each step. You can read it all or choose the topics that interest you most.

How Fat Rose from "Bad Guy" to "Miracle Nutrient" in Pop Culture Today

Here's the history of how the high-fat fads of today came into popularity: When we take food out of our diet, we have to replace it with something. When we found out that dietary fat was associated with heart disease in the 1950s, the American population didn't just decrease the amount of fat they were eating; they replaced it with foods containing higher amounts of sugar. This was for a variety of reasons, including to enhance the flavor that was lost when the fat was removed. It seems this is about the time we started overeating sugar.

High-fat diets have been coming and going for a long time. The most recent uptick in high-fat popularity was fueled in early 2016 when it became public knowledge that there was also research in the fifties revealing the problems of eating too much sugar and refined carbohydrates, but it was swept under the rug by lobbyists. This weakened public trust in the U.S. dietary standards and opened the door to even more extreme diets and nutrition conspiracy theories galore.

Extremists use these events to weaken trust in U.S. organizations who make the dietary guidelines, even though U.S. guidelines are congruent with those of other developed countries around the world. These associations, both in the U.S. and worldwide, are composed of thousands of educated people, studying and keeping abreast of the science. Fad diet proponents misuse the facts to support extreme points of view, including "everything you thought you knew about nutrition is now wrong." Now we have fads touting that we should eat more fat and cholesterol, including butter, bacon, and high-fat meats, despite the decades of research saying that these are foods we need to limit.

Current scientific evidence supports that *both* fat and sugar play a role in increasing the risk of cardiovascular disease, diabetes, obesity, and the speed of dementia. The majority of evidence still finds that those who eat more fruits, vegetables, legumes, and whole grains greatly reduce their risk for preventable disease and live a healthier, longer, and stronger life. Like you do now!

The News on Cholesterol and Eggs

Our bodies use cholesterol to produce hormones, vitamin D, and bile salts that help us digest fat. It's also an essential component of the insulating sheaths that cover nerve and brain cells. But as I said early on in this chapter, we don't need to focus on eating it to get the amounts that we need.

In the U.S. and other developed countries, there was a long-standing recommendation that we eat no more than 300 mg of cholesterol per day. But in the 2015 *Dietary Guidelines for Americans*, the U.S. removed the limits on dietary cholesterol. Despite what it may look like, what we know about cholesterol hasn't been totally turned upside down. We've just progressed! Here's what happened:

As far back as the nineteenth century, scientists knew that plaque in clogged arteries was partly made up of cholesterol. Cholesterol is typically found in foods that are also high in saturated fat. Because of this, when scientists were researching foods linked to heart disease, cholesterol and saturated fats have been studied as one.

In addition, cholesterol doesn't just "free float" in the blood; rather, it's bundled by the liver into small packages containing cholesterol, fats, and proteins. We call these lipoproteins, and they have different compositions and sizes. From smallest to largest they are HDL, LDL, IDL, VLDL, and chylomicrons. We'll talk about two of them here.

- HDL, the smallest particle, can remove fat and cholesterol from the artery walls, which is why they are often called "good" cholesterol or "healthy" cholesterol.

- LDL, the smallest of the four lipoproteins containing the highest amount of cholesterol, is most dangerous because it can damage artery walls. The damage, through a chain of events, can cause plaque buildup and high risk for heart disease and stroke. For this reason, LDLs are known as "bad" cholesterol.

The new view on cholesterol hasn't changed scientific opinion on LDL. But we've discovered the body's cholesterol regulation is much more influential than how much cholesterol we eat, when it comes to how much cholesterol we have in our blood. Experts around the globe still agree that diets high in saturated and trans fats are strongly associated with higher LDL. And there's evidence that, along with high saturated fat, eating too many simple carbs and sugar can also increase the levels of LDL in the blood, especially if you're sedentary and obese. So, that meal of a burger, fries, and a Coke can be worse than once thought, for some.

As you can see, the new guidelines aren't giving us license to have an eating frenzy with butter, cheese, bacon, and deep-fried food, like some diets are advocating. But eating lean proteins like lobster, shrimp, and eggs, that contain cholesterol are considered safe to eat.

Where to Find Fats

1. Trans fats are found in very small amounts in nature. More commonly they tend to occur in industrial processing when we turn liquid vegetable oils into solid forms in a process called hydrogenation. Hydrogenated oils can be found in processed food and deep-fried foods at restaurants and fast-food outlets. These oils are inexpensive and can be re-used many times in commercial fryers. There are regulations against using trans fats in processed food, but you still need to look at the labels and avoid *partially hydrogenated oil*.

Some countries and jurisdictions have restricted the use of trans fats in restaurants but not many. Right now, these places are Denmark, Switzerland, Canada, California, New York City, Baltimore, and Montgomery County, Maryland.

2. Saturated fat is a natural part of animal fat. You can

easily spot it because it's solid at room temperature, and it presents as white or marbling throughout the meat. Aside from fatty animal meat, it's in skin from chicken, turkey, or other birds. It's part of lard, cream, butter, cheese, and other full-fat dairy products; therefore, you'll also find it in baked goods. Three plant oils that contain saturated fats are coconut, palm, and palm kernel oils which are also abundant in processed foods.

3. Monounsaturated and polyunsaturated fats come from nuts, seeds, and their oils, as well as olives, avocados, and fatty fish like salmon. You can remember it like this: nuts, seeds, and OAFFS.

5. Omega-6 is an essential, polyunsaturated fat and found in almost every cooking oil we use today. If you eat out a lot, restaurants use plenty of oil. It's also found in animal fat. As a population, we have no problem getting omega-6.

6. Omega-3 is also an essential, polyunsaturated fat. In general, we tend not to get enough omega-3, which is why you may be hearing more about it in the media lately. Your best source of omega-3 is seafood. It's most abundant in fatty fish like salmon, tuna, mackerel, herring, sardines, bass, and trout. You can also find it in seaweed and algae.

As mentioned in chapter 5, you'll find small amounts of omega-3 in healthy meats. Grass-fed beef has almost twice as much as regular beef, because of the omega-3 in the grass. Organic chicken and their eggs may also have some omega-3 because of what they eat, and if they do, it'll be printed on the package. Milk and some yogurts can have added omega-3.

Tofu, soybeans, chia seeds, nuts, and seeds, and their oils also contain omega-3. Keep in mind that when you get omega-3 from plant sources, your body needs to further convert the plant form of omega-3 (ALA) into the forms that your body and brain use (DHA, EPA). Research finds the body is between 1%–15% percent efficient at this conversion. This means you need to eat at least 6.7 grams of plant omega-3 (ALA) to get one gram of DHA and EPA that you get from fish. So, fish is your most efficient source of omega-3 fat.

There's no standard amount of omega-3 in any fish. Like people, they have different lifestyles and eat different food, which will determine the amount and kind of fat they have on their bodies. In fact, studies have found that farm-raised fish, particularly salmon, have slightly more omega-3. Since they don't swim as much, they have more fat than wild fish.

The American Heart Association recommends about 8 ounces of fish per week for heart protection and more for those with heart disease and high triglycerides. If you're worried about mercury in fish, two to three servings per week is still considered safe by the FDA and the EPA. Children and pregnant women are advised to eat fish but avoid those highest in mercury, which are tilefish (golden bass or golden snapper), shark, swordfish, and king mackerel. Eat it baked, broiled, or steamed, and of course, not deep-fried.

Five-Star Restaurant Secrets

Here are some fat secrets that I use to make food incredibly flavorful while I feed and protect my brain and cardiovascular system at the same time.

> • Use high-quality, fresh oil *on top of* foods, like salad or pasta. High-quality olive oil will have a pungent flavor and taste like grass, lemon, or even butter. A little goes a long way, so you can splurge on great-tasting olive oil and it'll last a while. Adding it to your food after it's on your plate instead of during preparation will also help you use a lot less.

> • A little bit of cheese with deep, intense flavor goes far. Shave it lightly when using on top of foods.

> • You almost never need as much butter as you think. In cooking recipes, you can scale way back on butter and still get great flavor.

• When sautéing food in a pan, you only need a tablespoon of oil to start, especially when cooking with vegetables because they give off their own water to make juice.

• You don't need to use oil (or salt) when cooking pasta. Just stir it once or twice while cooking, so it doesn't stick together. Run hot water over it when it's done to get rid of the rest of the stickiness.

• Eat dessert from smaller containers and make it high quality when you do. For example, I put about 2 tablespoons of gelato in an espresso cup for dessert. If I want more, I get seconds with zero guilt. I'm totally satisfied, because eating this way makes a little feel like a lot. I enjoy gelato because it uses less cream (saturated fat) and more milk than normal ice cream, and it's high in flavor.

Easy Ways to Eat Healthy Fats
Here are some ideas for creatively eating more healthy fats daily:

• Use olive, nut, or seed oil when cooking.

• Use a high-flavor olive oil as a simple salad dressing.

• Add avocado to salads.

• Use avocado in sandwiches or wraps instead of mayonnaise.

• Try avocado on toast instead of butter once in a while.

• Add nuts to salads and grains for a nice crunch.

• Eat fish instead of meat several days per week.

How to Choose Lean Meats
Read the labels. For example, turkey burgers aren't guaranteed to be lower in fat or healthier than beef burgers. You might want to try bison, venison, or elk. These lean alternatives are

slowly entering the popular food markets.

If there's no label, remember that saturated fat is white in color and solid at room temperature. If you have a particularly fatty piece of meat, you can trim the fat with a knife before cooking to avoid cooking too much fat into the meat. If that's not an option, if you're at a restaurant for example, avoid eating most of it by cutting around it.

Avoid the Fads

It's especially important for you to avoid the fads because they're a waste of your time and energy as a leader. There's always a food group missing from fad diets that ultimately comes back around and proves to be necessary for optimal performance and energy. Besides, it's more motivating and energizing to choose the healthiest version possible of every food and continue to enjoy eating!

Take any chance you can to practice higher-level leadership conversation skills. Continue having inspiring conversations not only with others but also with yourself. Continue looking for ways you can easily maintain the healthy habits you've created here, and stay focused on being positive and productive and moving ahead.

Your exploration in food gets more fun and rewarding as you continue to experiment and perfect your systems. Head over to the Dietary Lifestyle Road Map where we'll put your whole experience together into your system, which will solidify your success. You've come a long way. I have no doubt that you'll keep progressing far into the future. Next, we'll touch on the one habit that's critical for you to be an inspiring and motivating leader for the long run.

| CHAPTER 7 |
FUELING YOUR MINDSET AND CELEBRATING SUCCESS

Now that much of your data gathering is done and your decisions are made regarding food choices, you only need to maintain these healthy practices so they become habits. As each day goes by, your habits become your life. And when you feed yourself regularly for energy, vitality, and health, life can be pretty great!

We just finished discussing how you can feed your brain so you can lead from the highest levels of health and energy. You also need to feed your brain for the right mindset, and you need to do it regularly. That will require something a little different than food.

Mindset

As a leader, with people looking to you for motivation, vision, innovation, and help with reaching goals, you're almost always in the spotlight. Ultimately, the responsibility is on you to keep yourself motivated and energized. The only way to do this day after day, authentically, is to stay focused on the positive.

Mindset is so important for motivation and success. If two sports teams with the exact same abilities play each other in a game, taking away any external, uncontrollable circumstances like wind blowing the ball in an unfortunate direction, the one with the best mindset wins. It's why coaches are known to give teams pep talks before games. It's why the best athletes are known to psych themselves up before every competition. It's that important.

Being a leader is like playing in a championship game every day. You have to perform well even when you encounter unexpected and extreme challenges, and you need to be mentally ready to do so. Great leaders give themselves pep talks and have routines and rituals to generate a positive mindset on a daily basis. At this time, you have a system for what to eat in the morning to feed your brain and body; you need to have a system to feed your mindset in the morning, too. You can *get your mind right to start your day right,* and it can be incredibly powerful when you do so.

I know, mornings can be tough. And since creativity takes mental energy, you can rely on outside sources to help you rev up your brain and start your day thinking positively. There are many places to get a dose of positive energy: books, audiobooks, podcasts, or channels on YouTube. You can envision a positive day ahead while you meditate, do a few simple yoga poses, or pray. At the very least, you can do it while you shower or commute to work. Make it a simple and easy part of your morning system that you look forward to. Exercise is great for producing energy and positivity in that it increases adrenaline and endorphins, but it's not the same as what I'm talking about here. You must purposefully train your mind to think positively, although it can indeed be done while exercising as well. Evoking a positive mindset first thing, along with eating foods that provide your body and mind with clean, long-burning fuel will take you far into a good day. Good days add up to great weeks, and months, and years, and create your success as leader. Take it a day at a time.

What and Why

It's the end of your journey in this book, but healthy eating is a never-ending, exciting journey! There's always more to learn, experience, and enjoy when it comes to food. You now have a solid foundation to build on. You have what you need to avoid the fads and stay on track for optimal performance with long-term success. And you can do that no matter where your leadership life takes you—the office cafeteria, another country, or your kitchen. In general, here's a recap of what you need to do:

- Eat as many clean fruits and vegetables as possible to get your brain-boosting, body-vitalizing nutrients. Make half of your meal with them whenever you possibly can.

- Eat the right kind of carbs for fuel and to maintain a healthy brain and gut microbiome. Eat grain-based foods, whole grains, and root vegetables as a quarter of your meal.

- Eat lean, healthy protein, and make it another quarter of your meals and snacks. Avoid processed meats and fast-food meats. If you're a vegan or vegetarian, eat the largest variety of vegetables possible, vary your grains, and vary your protein sources of legumes and legume products.

- Focus on your healthy fat intake by adding salmon and more fish to your diet. Drizzle some healthy oil on top of salads and accessorize your meals with avocados, nuts, and seeds.

- Drink more water, less soda, and less high-calorie coffee drinks to keep your mind running smoothly all day without energy crashes and residual fatigue. Eat regularly to stoke your metabolism and fuel your brain—but not too much to slow yourself down.

There you have it! What we know about food and diet is based on years of research that only builds on itself. These are the eating habits that research finds will help keep your DNA younger than your actual age. This is the way to eat for anti-inflammatory, immune-boosting, disease-resisting, cancer-fighting effects. These are the magic ingredients that will keep your skin looking fresh and youthful, your eyes bright and working well, and protect your brain from degradation. If you're doing all of the above, you'll be feeling and performing incredibly well, and set to have a strong and vibrant future.

Stay Grounded

My advice for keeping your sanity and staying grounded and keeping a good mindset for healthy nutrition practices is to ignore most of what you see in the media about food. Ignore information on social media, which is mostly advertisements in disguise, made to drag you onto the next roller coaster of diets for the sake of profits. Be wary of actors on commercials in white coats, posing as doctors. Take lightly the news, magazine articles, television shows, and movies that express only the opinions of passionate, well-meaning people who are untrained in the nutrition profession. Be curious when someone says they've "researched" a subject, which can mean a couple of hours on Google.

When it comes to professionals you can trust for nutrition, you'll get the best return on investment with someone who has a formal education in the field from a reputable university and credentials. Experience is a plus. In case you didn't know, most doctors receive no education in nutrition. When they do, it's usually a couple of weeks or a couple of months at best. Doctors have important knowledge in the areas in which they've studied and work, and you can depend on them to help you in their specific areas of expertise. If you have a health issue that you want to address with nutrition, it's always important to talk to your physician—and ask for a referral to a nutrition professional who can help you with the details.

Eating well is one of the best forms of prevention to keep you from needing medicine in the first place. If you want to keep up with the newest information and research, find true professionals in the field who you can trust for guidance. Ask them questions, even pay them to work with you until you get the hang of it on your own.

Remember that science doesn't flip on a dime. We know a lot now about how the human body works. We have a huge foundation upon which we're building. Watch out for people who claim to be the "only person" who is telling you the truth and that everyone else is either lying or doesn't know what they're talking about. The U.S. and many other developed countries have thousands of scientists and professionals researching and discussing how to eat optimally in today's world. The likelihood of one person or a small, fringe group "figuring it all out" by themselves is incredibly low. If you want to double-check your sources, look at any American or European agency's official health websites for their current policies and standards, many of which I list in the References. And remember, the data that you gathered here about yourself will always be an important piece of the picture when it comes to making your best decisions about food.

Your Final Step—for Now

By this time, you've taken steps that'll add up to a big difference in your energy, mood, decision making, brainpower, productivity, patience, creativity, and ultimately, your ability to lead. The final step in this part of your journey is to take a look back and see how far you've come. I'm willing to bet you've come a long way!

Wrap up your transformational journey with a second look at your initial data, since numbers don't lie. In chapter 1, you took some measurements and now it's time to take them again. Get as many measurements as possible and write them in the chart you started in your Dynamic Lifestyle Road Map, Step 1. It'll be exciting and motivating for you to see that you've changed for the better. Nothing surpasses having hard data about your own improvement. And you just might even see more improvement than you expected. Observing your successes, no matter how large or small, is a powerful way to feed your positive mindset, and it will motivate you to keep moving forward with your healthy food choices.

Maximize Your Opportunities for Success

Life changes. Our bodies change. Circumstances change. When change happens, we may need to change our food choices too. You can always do that in a smart and grounded way by gathering data, listening to your body, and building on the knowledge you have here.

You'll need to keep stretching and thinking outside the box to keep healthy food habits in a world that's forever pulling you toward unhealthy choices. But keep your integrity with yourself; keep following your systems, and it'll pay off immeasurably. Extreme good health is not a luxury for you; it's a necessity if you want to keep going at a high pace, producing the highest-level results for the long haul. You can choose food that serves you. You can create the small amount of time and energy it takes to make it happen. It's worth it.

Along with eating to benefit your mind and body, invest daily in visualizing your ideal future. Keep reinventing conversations with yourself to create a mindset that sustains your positive energy and motivates you. Listen not only to your mind but your body too, when it comes to making good decisions. Getting better-acquainted with your intuition yields enormous returns and will serve you in all your choices, including food.

Celebrate

This is just the beginning of your healthy, diet-free, enjoyable exploration of food and how it can help you be the best leader that you can be. You can visit EatToLead.com for additional motivation and guidance from me. I'll share supplemental information over there, bust myths as they come out, and let you know when I'm offering events in your area or online. Make sure to get on my mailing list if you want my most current material to come right to your in-box.

You may have inferred from your reading here that exercise is another key to mastering your energy and your leadership life. At some point, you may hear your body ask for more exercise. If so, I offer guidance on exercise for the leader too, which I'll also share on the website.

Do something nice for yourself and celebrate your accomplishments. Celebrating success, no matter how small or large, is important. It gives us motivation to keep moving forward. It also provides us with good experience and good memories—and that's the good stuff in life. If you loved the results you got from this journey, I'd love to hear about your success. Contact me at EatToLead.com and we can celebrate your accomplishments together!

Congratulations!

| THE DYNAMIC LIFESTYLE ROAD MAP™ |

How It Works

This is where you'll bring your knowledge out of your mind and into reality. Come here after each chapter, and I'll lead you through making some comfortable goals based on what you just read. I'll guide you in taking notes throughout the week to get data on whether your changes are working. And I'll help you make sense of your notes once you're done. This is how we'll create your personal food system that supports your individual needs and your optimal performance, in leadership as well as in life.

If you need more pages than I offer here, you can download them at EatToLead.com. Now, let's get started!

Dynamic Lifestyle Road Map Foundations for Success—What's Your Why?

What are the deepest, most personal reasons you want to change your eating habits? Write it all here. Include not only how changing your eating habits for the better will benefit you but also how it'll impact those around you—from colleagues to family and friends. Turn to the next page for the second foundational question.

Revisit this page often.

What are your strengths? Write down some of your personal qualities that usually help you overcome roadblocks in life. Most likely you draw upon these strengths to be the best leader that you can be. You can look to your strengths to succeed in this journey too. Write them here.

Revisit this page often too.

Dynamic Lifestyle Road Map Step 1—Gathering Initial Data

The more data you have, the better positioned you are to observe whether your food decisions are serving you well. You may be looking at the scale for signs of physical improvement and progress. But the scale measures only one aspect of all the ways your body can change for the better. More information is definitely needed.

Along with journaling, it's well worth it to take some measurements to get an accurate picture of your progress. There can be big changes in these before-and-after numbers once you've taken the steps in this book. The positive results that can show up in this data can keep you motivated far into the future.

The measurements below are in order of least to most time-consuming to take and get. I describe how to take the measurements below—get as many as you can. There's a second column for you to write your "after" numbers.

1. *Current weight.* Weigh yourself on a scale in the morning (ideally after your first trip to the bathroom but before eating breakfast). Weight is the easiest measurement to take. The scale, by no means, tells the whole story of your physical state. Get this measurement only as a piece of the whole picture.

2. *Current body fat percentage.* Home scales that measure body fat can be pretty accurate these days. Even if it's not 100% accurate, measuring with the same tool will give you the data to know whether you're going up or down and by how much.

3. *Resting heart rate.* Resting heart rate is best done in the morning, just after waking without an alarm, sitting on your bed if possible. You can use a watch with a heart rate monitor or do it yourself.

To take your own heart rate, place your index and middle finger of your right hand onto the major artery at the bottom of your wrist (right below your thumb) on your left hand. (The best way is to come around from behind, with the palm of your right hand on the top of your left wrist.) Press just firmly enough to feel the pulse but not firm enough to stop the beat. Count the beats of your pulse for one minute. Write it down.

The American Heart Association says that 60 to 100 beats per minute is normal. The healthier your heart is, the lower your resting heart rate will be. Athletes have resting heart rates as low as 40 beats per minute.

4. *Circumferences.* In terms of measuring changes to your outward appearance, these are great measurements too. As your body shifts for the better it may not show on the scale, but it can show significantly in your circumference measurements.

Using a measuring tape, measure the right side of your body:

Arm 1: biggest part of your bicep (flexed)

Arm 2: biggest part of your bicep (relaxed)

Chest and Back 1: across the center of your breastbone

Chest and Back 2: largest part of your chest, which may be different from measurement above

Waist 1: smallest part of your waist

Waist 2: largest part of your waist

Hips: largest part of your hips (below your belly button, across your hip bones)

Glutes: largest part of your rear (usually somewhere close to the lower area)

Upper Leg: top of your leg, right below your glutes

Calf: largest part of your calf

5. *Resting blood pressure.* It's best to have a professional do this. The automatic cuffs we get in the pharmacy can work, but sometimes they don't. And when they don't, they *really* misread. To avoid inaccurate, high-blood pressure readings, sit down and relax for at least 10 minutes before getting the

reading. During the blood pressure test, relax your entire body. Imagine yourself at a quiet, calm beach or any place that's relaxing for you. Release all the tension from your muscles and breathe long and deep.

6. *Blood lipids.* These include HDL, LDL, VDL, and VLDL. These tests need to be scheduled in advance as they're taken in a doctor's office. They're taken by a blood draw specifically after you've fasted overnight. This will tell you how much fat and cholesterol are floating in your blood.

7. *Fasting glucose.* This test also requires a blood draw and requires that you fast for twelve hours. You can take this test along with that for blood lipids above. It tells you whether your blood glucose is being processed normally in your body.

Data Worth Collecting:	Date 1:	Date 2:
Weight		
Resting heart rate		
Body fat percentage		
Circumferences		
Arm 1		
Arm 2		
Chest and Back 1		
Chest and Back 2		
Waist 1		
Waist 2		
Hips		
Glutes		
Upper Leg		
Calf		
Resting blood pressure		
Blood lipids		
Glucose tolerance and/or fasting glucose		

Gathering Data Through Journaling

In the following pages, you'll journal about the food you're eating. Write the date and the time, what you ate, and how much you ate. This will all matter when it comes time to look back on your notes to draw some conclusions.

Of equal importance is that you pause before and after eating and determine how you feel physically and mentally. Are you feeling energized? Sleepy? Angry? Sad? Positive? Neutral? Starving? Stuffed? Every physical and mental feeling before and after you eat is a clue that leads to creating your best eating plan. You'll start to see patterns for your best and worst times to eat, the best and worst foods for you to eat, what provides you with energy, and what takes it away.

Good times to take note are before and after you eat and at the beginning and end of each day. Also, note obvious slumps or highs throughout the day. Write everything you think matters and be completely honest with yourself.

The notes are flexible enough for you to freeform-write as much as you need. For example, in the food section, you might write: *Monday, 7:15 a.m., 2 bowls of cereal.* And next to it, in the observation section, you might write: *Woke up at 6 a.m. and needed more sleep. After breakfast, felt tired, needed coffee.* Use the sections in whatever way they work best for you. To get an idea of the amount of food you're eating, which I highly recommend, see "If You Don't Have Measuring Tools" in The Leading Edge section.

Quiet times are when we hear our intuition best. Take some time before or after your meals to be still and listen to your body. See what comes up in your intuition not only about food but also about anything else happening in your day. Write notes on this too. Writing more in your journal is always better than less, because we never know what information will be useful in the future. If you need more pages or want to keep your journaling separate, you can download these sheets at EatToLead.com.

Date/Time/Food I Ate	Observations (Physical, Mental, Sleep, Mood)

Next Week's Food Choices

While journaling, you may come up with some new and improved meal ideas. Make note of any ideas for improvement here so you can implement them next week. *Not this week!*

-

-

-

-

-

-

-

-

-

Date/Time/Food I Ate	Observations (Physical, Mental, Sleep, Mood)

Date/Time/Food I Ate	Observations (Physical, Mental, Sleep, Mood)

Looking Back

Let's put your data to use. Now that you've journaled for a week, take a look back at what you've written. What are your top discoveries or conclusions? Try to find at least three.

-
-
-
-
-
-
-
-

Dynamic Lifestyle Road Map Step 2—Goals and the Most Important Thing

In Step 1, you gathered some initial data points. You've created a very strong foundation for success. Let's build on it now and create some goals.

Based on last week's information and conclusions, make two or three goals that are in line with your "Why" and make them SMART. A smart goal for our purposes is: Specific, Measurable, Attainable, Rewarding, and Time-Bound. Here are some details on why making smart goals is smart.

1. *Specific.* Make these goals as specific as possible. This is the concrete evidence you'll have at the end of these six steps that will show your progress. Here are some examples: eating a balanced breakfast five days per week, bringing lunch to work at least one day per week, drinking eight glasses of water per day, getting eight hours of sleep at night, eliminating afternoon slumps, and exercising daily.

After taking your physical measurements you might get a few ideas about what you'd like those numbers to be in the future. If so, make some specific goals around your measurements too.

2. *Measurable.* Whatever your goals are, make sure they're something you'll be measuring or journaling about so you have data. All my clients make progress, but many of them are so hard on themselves that if we didn't keep measurements and numbers, they'd never believe they were getting anywhere. We rely on numbers to see whether our company or business is making progress; numbers are equally necessary to evaluate our progress in life if we're serious about it.

3. *Attainable.* Make sure your goals are realistically attainable in the timeframe you've set.

4. *Rewarding.* Make sure your goals are important enough to you that they'll make a positive difference for you when you reach them.

5. *Time-Bound.* Having a set amount of time to reach a goal

is always more motivating and helps us stay focused. As I mentioned in the introduction, give yourself at least a week for each step (not less) to let new habits take hold.

Write the date by which you want to have finished this book and your transformational journey below. Add two or three smart goals that you'd like to have accomplished by the time you're through.

By this date: _____

I will:

1.

2.

3.

Journaling Your Data on Vegetables

Take a look at the initial data you took in Step 1. Have you been eating at least three servings of vegetables each day? If not, it's time to ramp it up this week.

You can simply log only the vegetables you eat or continue logging all the foods you eat. The benefit from logging all food is that it will give you more complete data. If you're using an app and log everything, you'll see how your calories go down and your nutrition goes up when you add more vegetables.

Focus on thinking outside the box to get many different colorful, nutrient-rich vegetables in your lunches and dinners. Keep track of your energy levels, moods, sleep, and anything else you want data for. If you need more pages, you can get them at EatToLead.com.

Planning Brainstorm

Brainstorm while your mind is still focused on the new food choices you'll make this week. Before journaling, answer the following:

To what meals can I easily add more vegetables?

When and where?

Which vegetables?

How can I make this easy and enjoyable?

Date/Time/Food I Ate (Focus on vegetables)	Observations (Physical, Mental, Sleep, Mood)

Go-to Vegetables

Go-to Vegetables are the vegetables you'll want to have stocked on a regular basis in your refrigerator, cupboards, office, and elsewhere. They're also the meals you find at restaurants that fit your criteria. While you're observing your body and brain's responses to food this week, write the vegetable dishes and meals with vegetables that you like and want to repeat.

Review the list to quickly decide where to eat or use it as part of your grocery list. In the final steps, these lists will help jog your memory to create your optimal meal systems.

Home   Restaurant

Date/Time/Food I Ate (Focus on vegetables)	Observations (Physical, Mental, Sleep, Mood)

Date/Time/Food I Ate (Focus on vegetables)	Observations (Physical, Mental, Sleep, Mood)

Looking Back

Now that you've journaled for at least a week, take a look at your notes. What discoveries or conclusions can you make? Try to find at least three.

-

-

-

-

-

-

-

-

-

Dynamic Lifestyle Road Map Step 3—
Journaling Your Data on Fruit

You're creating a system that's uniquely yours; one that's easy and enjoyable for you. In this step, you'll focus on fruit in breakfast and snacks. You're collecting data on *new* information once again, so it's ideal to observe how these specific changes affect how you feel and perform while you're making the changes. If you're using an app and documenting all your food, you'll once again see your nutrition go up and calories go down as you start swapping sweets for fruit.

Take a look at your journaling in Step 1 to see how much fruit you were eating daily. Were you eating two servings of fruit and eating fruit when you wanted sweets? If not, it's time to get to that goal.

Keep track of your energy levels, moods, sleep, and anything else you want to understand more thoroughly. Also notice when you have integrity with yourself, especially when eating right is difficult. Make notes about that too. It's important to acknowledge your successes. If you need more pages, you can get them at EatToLead.com.

Planning Brainstorm

Brainstorm now while your mind is still focused on your food choices this week. Make your food choices easier by answering the following:

To what meals can I easily add fruit?

What will I eat for breakfast this week?

How can I make my snacks healthier?

How can I make this easy and fun?

Date/Time/Food I Ate (Focus on breakfast and snacks)	Observations (Physical, Mental, Sleep, Mood)

Go-to Fruit

Use this section to write down fruit that you liked and want to have regularly on hand. Write what you'd like to keep at home and the restaurant and corresponding dish you liked when eating out. This is part of your personal system.

Home	Restaurant

Date/Time/Food I Ate (Focus on breakfast and snacks)	Observations (Physical, Mental, Sleep, Mood)

Date/Time/Food I Ate (Focus on breakfast and snacks)	Observations (Physical, Mental, Sleep, Mood)

Looking Back

Now that you're done journaling for at least a week, take a look at your notes and write down your top discoveries or conclusions from this step. Try to think of at least three. Include what you found to be your ideal breakfasts and snacks at this time.

-
-
-
-
-
-
-
-
-

Dynamic Lifestyle Road Map Step 4—Journaling Your Data on Carbs

This step is about carbohydrates and your energy levels. Focus on carbs and observe your energy before and after mealtimes and in between. If you're changing your eating habits in this step, this is additional, new information and you'll want to capture it here. You may want to observe how many hours you can go and still be optimal in between meals. Also notice what kinds of carbohydrates work best for your energy levels in the morning, afternoon, and evening. Keep watch on how you're sleeping and your moods. If you need more pages, you can get them at EatToLead.com.

Planning Brainstorm

Brainstorm here while your mind is still focused on carbs, so you can get a head start on succeeding this week.

In what meals can I substitute healthier carb-dense foods for less healthy carbs?

What new carb-dense foods can I try this week?

When and where?

How can I make this easy and fun?

Date/Time/Food I Ate (Focus on the carbohydrate sources in your meals)	Observations (Physical, Mental, Sleep, Mood)

Go-to Carbs

While you're observing this week, make a list of your go-to carbs and carb meals here. What healthy carbs would you like to eat regularly, make you feel good, and provide you with the right kind of energy at the right times of the day? What carbs will you have on hand at home and in the office? What restaurants and what dishes do they serve that you'll be eating regularly? Soon, you'll be able to copy and paste your success over and over and make a system of it. Better yet, you'll make a habit of it.

Home   Restaurant

Date/Time/Food I Ate (Focus on the carbohydrate sources in your meals)	Observations (Physical, Mental, Sleep, Mood)

Date/Time/Food I Ate (Focus on the carbohydrate sources in your meals)	Observations (Physical, Mental, Sleep, Mood)

Looking Back

Now that you're done with the week, take a brief look back at your notes. Write at least three discoveries or conclusions you can make from them. Include what you've found to be ideal carbs and the best times to eat them.

-

-

-

-

-

-

-

-

-

Dynamic Lifestyle Road Map Step 5—Journaling Your Data on Protein

Journal your food and focus on what proteins you eat and how it makes you feel. To see if you're getting the amount you need, tally up your protein for a few days and compare those amounts to your calculations in The Leadership Edge section.

After journaling this week, we'll start bringing all your work in this road map together in the Modular Meals™ exercise at the end. As always, if you need more pages, you can get them at EatToLead.com.

Visioning

Do some future visioning around your goals to eat better. This is how we stay highly driven and progressing toward all our goals—in our personal life as well as career. I've got some space here for you to play with the exercise: Start by envisioning yourself at three different time points in the future. Then, write a time by which you'd like to realize your vision (i.e., two months, one year, five years, etc.) and write a bold, positive vision of yourself.

In _____time, I will be:

In _____time, I will be:

In _____time, I will be:

Planning Brainstorm

Brainstorm here while your mind is still focused on how you can eat healthier proteins, and enough protein.

In what meals will I substitute healthy protein for less healthy protein?

How much protein do I need and how will I get it?

When and where will I eat it?

How will I make this easy and enjoyable?

Date/Time/Food I Ate (Focus on the protein in your meals)	Observations (Physical, Mental, Sleep, Mood)

Go-to Proteins

While observing this week, make your list of go-to proteins. These are protein foods that you like, find easy to eat, and want to have on hand, both at work and at home. Include meals you've eaten out that you want to eat on a regular basis.

Home	Restaurant

Date/Time/Food I Ate (Focus on the protein in your meals)	Observations (Physical, Mental, Sleep, Mood)

Date/Time/Food I Ate (Focus on the protein in your meals)	Observations (Physical, Mental, Sleep, Mood)

Looking Back

Now that you're done with the week, take a brief look back at your notes. What are your top discoveries or conclusions?

-

-

-

-

-

-

-

-

-

Modular Meals™

This is a system I call Modular Meals. Here's how it works. Look at meals as three separate modules: (1) fruit/vegetables, (2) protein, and (3) carbs. Think of how you'd plan your wardrobe for a business trip where all the tops, bottoms, and shoes mix and match. If you do it right, you can mix clothes and have many outfits that work for the weather, the event you're attending, even your mood. Now you'll do the same with food.

Let's do an exercise around dinner. To make this fast and easy, use the foods from the go-to foods you listed in each step. We'll start with the protein—pick four different, healthy proteins that you like and write them in the table below. Then, think up eight healthy vegetables that you like for dinner and write them down. If you have to repeat a vegetable because there are eight lines to fill in, that's fine. Finally, choose four stand-alone carbohydrate sources that you liked to eat from the last step and write them down.

Proteins
1.
2.
3.
4.

Fruits/Vegetables
1.
2.
3.
4.
5.
6.
7.
8.

Carbohydrates
1.
2.
3.
4.

Now, randomly pick one protein, two vegetables, and one carbohydrate from the lists above, and write them next to number one through four below. If you've been following along with the information I've been sharing and putting it into action in your life, you no doubt can see that all of these very simple food items go together easily as mix-and-match foods. If you're grocery shopping, the items on the above list can be the items that you shop for and put together at home. You can mix and match the components from a restaurant menu just as well. You can easily mix and match for snacks too. You can create great meals with high-quality components and rotate the components to keep it interesting and satisfying. We can combine them depending on our mood, or even the weather, just like clothes.

1.

2.

3.

4.

Here are four of my personal favorites from home:

- Baked salmon, spinach salad with balsamic dressing, and pasta with lemony olive oil.

- A wrap filled with any protein, orange and red peppers, dark greens, and brown rice. This also makes a great meal bowl.

- Lean red meat; a potato or yam with plain yogurt on top; and a tomato, avocado, and cucumber salad.

- Stir-fry with any protein and almost any vegetable I have in my fridge. I pair that with sauce and rice or pasta.

Here are four of my local restaurant favorites:

- Chicken or seafood dumplings with sides of steamed mushrooms and bok choy.

- Quiche with a mixed green salad or fruit salad.

- Sushi with edamame and seaweed salad.

- Soft tacos with grilled protein, shredded cabbage and carrots, with a side of multicolored rice.

Write down four meal combinations before moving on. It's a good time to use some of your notes from the last couple of weeks. See whether you want to repeat any meals you've already eaten with just a little tweak here or there. Some people do very well rotating four or five simple meal combinations throughout the week and eating their favorites over and over again. I do too.

Dynamic Lifestyle Road Map Step 6—Journaling Your Data on Fat

Are you curious to know how much fat you're eating now or had been eating? You can easily find out by taking a look at the last few weeks that you logged your foods. You know enough about fat now to identify foods that have fats and whether they're healthy or unhealthy.

Start choosing healthier fats in your meals if you haven't already. Log your meals and how you felt before and after meals, at the beginning and end of your day. Take some time before or after your meals to be still and pay attention to the conversations you're having with yourself. Quiet times are the best way to observe your thoughts and, if needed, take a moment to gently guide yourself into more positive, forward-thinking, and inspiring self-talk. Circle back around to put all your findings into "Your Meal System" at the end of this step. If you need more pages, you can get them at EatToLead.com.

Planning Brainstorm

Brainstorm here while your mind is still focused on how you can eat healthier fat.

Where might I be eating an excess of saturated fat or unhealthy fat?

How can I swap less healthy fat with fats that are healthier?

How will I get my weekly omega-3s?

How will I make this easy and enjoyable?

Date/Time/Food I Ate (Focus on fat in your meals)	Observations (Physical, Mental, Sleep, Mood)

Leadership Conversations

Take note of some conversations you're currently having that aren't productive, forward-thinking, or inspiring when it comes to making the best food choices.

Based on the above notes, write down some phrases you can say instead that are productive, forward-thinking, and inspiring. Repeat them to yourself whenever you notice yourself going down the old mental pathways about food.

Date/Time/Food I Ate (Focus on fat in your meals)	Observations (Physical, Mental, Sleep, Mood)

Date/Time/Food I Ate (Focus on fat in your meals)	Observations (Physical, Mental, Sleep, Mood)

Looking Back

Now that you're done with the week, take a brief look back at your notes. What are your top discoveries or conclusions? Find at least three.

-

-

-

-

-

-

-

-

Your Meal System

This is your system for success. Write down your favorite meals and snacks that include proteins, carbs, fruit/vegetables, and healthy fat. These will be your go-to meals—the meals you choose regularly that support your energy, brain power, mood, mental acuity, physical strength, and health. They'll make it easy for you to have the stamina and fortitude to be the leader that you want to be now and long into the future. You'll use the list for grocery shopping, as well as choosing restaurants. You'll eat these meals more regularly than others, because success is what you do 90% of the time. Your list will change a little, and grow a little, as you continue to explore and experiment. Get ready for your next level of leadership performance. The benefits you get from this don't stop now; they keep coming!

Meal Combinations

Include protein, carb, fruit/vegetables, and healthy fat in each. Include meals you eat at restaurants as well as those you'll eat at home.

Favorite Breakfasts

Best Lunches/Snacks

Best Dinners

The Final Step

Looking Back on the Big Picture

Celebrating success gives you power to keep moving forward. Looking at the data you've collected from beginning to end, what are your top-three biggest successes? How does it feel to have made these accomplishments? Linger on this for a moment. Allow yourself to feel pride in your success and joy for the positive, brighter future that you've created for yourself, those you lead, and everyone else in your life.

I'm proud of you for completing this journey, and you should be proud of yourself. As I've said many times before, if this were easy, everyone would have a healthy diet. Let me know about your successes, if you'd like, at EatToLead.com. I'd love to hear from you!

1. What I accomplished:

How it feels:

How I see this impacting my future:

2. What I accomplished:

How it feels:

How I see this impacting my future:

3. What I accomplished:

How it feels:

How I see this impacting my future:

| REFERENCES |

Introduction
Blackburn, Elizabeth H., and Elissa Epel. *The Telomere Effect: A Revolutionary Approach to Living Younger, Healthier, Longer*. New York: Grand Central Publishing, 2018.

Bloem, Craig. "Why Successful People Wear the Same Thing Every Day." Inc.com. February 20, 2018. https://www.inc.com/craig-bloem/this-1-unusual-habit-helped-make-mark-zuckerberg-steve-jobs-dr-dre-successful.html.

Burchard, Brendon. *High Performance Habits: How Extraordinary People Become That Way*. Carlsbad: Hay House, Inc., 2017.

Corbyn, Zoë. "Elizabeth Blackburn on the Telomere Effect: 'It's about Keeping Healthier for Longer,'" January 29, 2017. https://www.theguardian.com/science/2017/jan/29/telomere-effect-elizabeth-blackburn-nobel-prize-medicine-chromosomes.

Croll, Pauline H., Trudy Voortman, M. Arfan Ikram, Oscar H. Franco, Josje D. Schoufour, Daniel Bos, and Meike W. Vernooij. "Better Diet Quality Relates to Larger Brain Tissue Volumes," June 12, 2018. http://n.neurology.org/content/early/2018/05/16/WNL.0000000000005691.

Freedman, David H. "How to Fix the Obesity Crisis." *Scientific American* 304, no. 2 (2011): 40–47. https://doi.org/10.1038/scientificamerican0211-40.

Mayer, Emeran A. *The Mind-Gut Connection: How the Hidden Conversation within Our Bodies Impacts Our Mood, Our Choices, and Our Overall Health*. New York: Harper Wave, 2018.

Pelley, John. "Making Active Learning Effective." *Medical Science Educator* 24, no. S1 (2014): 13–18. https://doi.org/10.1007/s40670-014-0087-1.

Rock, David. *Your Brain at Work: Strategies for Overcoming Distraction, Regaining Focus and Working Smarter All Day Long*. New York: Harper Collins, 2010.

Sinek, Simon. *Start with Why: How Great Leaders Inspire Everyone to Take Action*. London, England: Penguin Business, 2019.

Weinhold, Bob. "Epigenetics: The Science of Change." *Environmental Health Perspectives* 114, no. 3 (2006). https://doi.org/10.1289/ehp.114-a160.

Chapter 1
Coughlin, Janelle W., Phillip J. Brantley, Catherine M. Champagne, William M. Vollmer, Victor J. Stevens, Kristine Funk, Arlene T. Dalcin, et al. "The Impact of Continued Intervention on Weight: Five-Year Results from the Weight Loss Maintenance Trial." *Obesity* 24, no. 5 (2016): 1046–53. https://doi.org/10.1002/oby.21454.

Csikszentmihalyi, Mihaly. *Good Business: Leadership, Flow, and the Making of Meaning*. New York: Penguin Books, 2004.

Economy, Peter. "The 9 Leadership Traits That Encourage Your Team to Succeed," January 24, 2014.

https://www.inc.com/peter-economy/the-9-traits-that-define-great-leadership.html.

Freedman, David H. "How to Fix the Obesity Crisis." *Scientific American* 304, no. 2 (2011): 40–47. https://doi.org/10.1038/scientificamerican0211-40.

"Correct Portion Sizes: How to Keep Portion Distortion in Check." HealthyEating.org, n.d. https://www.healthyeating.org/Healthy-Eating/Healthy-Living/Weight-Management/Article-Viewer/article/348/correct-portion-sizes-how-to-keep-portion-distortion-in-check#.XH15FQVfGVc.link.

Hollis, Jack F., Christina M. Gullion, Victor J. Stevens, Phillip J. Brantley, Lawrence J. Appel, Jamy D. Ard, Catherine M. Champagne, et al. "Weight Loss During the Intensive Intervention Phase of the Weight-Loss Maintenance Trial." *American Journal of Preventive Medicine* 35, no. 2 (2008): 118–26. https://doi.org/10.1016/j.amepre.2008.04.013.

Kase, Larina. "Great Leaders Are Great Decision-Makers - A Peer-Reviewed Academic Articles | GBR." October 29, 2017. https://gbr.pepperdine.edu/2010/10/great-leaders-are-great-decision-makers/.

"Keeping A Food Diary Doubles Diet Weight Loss, Study Suggests." July 8, 2008. https://www.sciencedaily.com/releases/2008/07/080708080738.htm.

"NCI Dictionary of Cancer Terms." n.d. https://www.cancer.gov/publications/dictionaries/cancer-terms/def/nutrient-dense-food.

O'Connor, Carol A. *Secrets of Great Leaders: 50 Ways to Make a Difference*. London: John Murray Learning, 2015.

Rock, David. *Quiet Leadership–Six Steps to Transforming Performance at Work; Help People Think Better–Don't Tell Them What to Do!* New York, NY: Harper, 2006.

Stanier, Michael Bungay. *The Coaching Habit: Say Less, Ask More & Change the Way You Lead Forever*. Toronto, Ont.: Box of Crayons Press, 2016.

Tamir, Diana I., and Jason P. Mitchell. "Disclosing information about the self is intrinsically rewarding." May 22, 2012. https://www.pnas.org/content/109/21/8038.full.

"WebMD Portion and Size Guide – Portion-Size Guide." WebMD, 2019. https://www.webmd.com/diet/printable/wallet-portion-control-size-guide.

Zenger, John H., and Joe Folkman. *Speed: How Leaders Accelerate Successful Execution*. McGraw-Hill, 2017.

Chapter 2

Blackburn, Elizabeth H., and Elissa Epel. *The Telomere Effect: A Revolutionary Approach to Living Younger, Healthier, Longer*. New York: Grand Central Publishing, 2018.

Csikszentmihalyi, Mihaly. *Flow: The Psychology of Optimal Experience*. Harper Perennial Modern Classics, 2008.

Gabel, Luci. "Striving for Higher Goals in Life? Expect to Fail, and Welcome It." LuciFit, October 8, 2018.

http://lucifit.com/striving-for-higher-goals-in-life-expect-to-fail-and-welcome-it/.

Hammond, Billy R., L. Stephen Miller, Medina O. Bello, Cutter A. Lindbergh, Catherine Mewborn, and Lisa M. Renzi-Hammond. "Effects of Lutein/Zeaxanthin Supplementation on the Cognitive Function of Community Dwelling Older Adults: A Randomized, Double-Masked, Placebo-Controlled Trial." *Frontiers in Aging Neuroscience* 9 (2017). https://doi.org/10.3389/fnagi.2017.00254.

Katz, David L., and Mark Bittman. *The Truth about Food: Why Pandas Eat Bamboo and People Get Bamboozled*. New York, NY: Dystel & Goderich Literary Management, 2018.

Mayer, Emeran A. *The Mind-Gut Connection: How the Hidden Conversation within Our Bodies Impacts Our Mood, Our Choices, and Our Overall Health*. Harper Collins, 2016.

Morris, Martha Clare. *Diet for the MIND: The Latest Science on What to Eat to Prevent Alzheimer's and Cognitive Decline*. Little, Brown and Company, 2017.

"Report on Nutrient Losses and Gains Factors Used in European Food Composition Databases." April 2006. https://www.ars.usda.gov/ARSUserFiles/80400525/Data/retn/retno6.pdf.

Sanli, S. G., E. D. Kizilkanat, N. Boyan, E. T. Ozsahin, M. G. Bozkir, R. Soames, H. Erol, and O. Oguz. "Stature Estimation Based on Hand Length and Foot Length." November 2005. https://www.ncbi.nlm.nih.gov/pubmed/16187319.

"Serving Size Chart." US Dairy Council, 2014.
https://www.healthyeating.org/Portals/0/Documents/School
s/Parent Ed/Portion_Sizes_Serving_Chart.pdf.

Slavin, Joanne. "Fiber and Prebiotics: Mechanisms and Health
Benefits." *Nutrients* 5, no. 4 (2013): 1417–35.
https://doi.org/10.3390/nu5041417.

USDA. (2007, December). *Nutrient Retention Factors* [PDF].
Beltsville Human Nutrition Research Center: Nutrient Data
Library.
https://www.ars.usda.gov/ARSUserFiles/80400525/Data/ret
n/retno6.pdf.

Vishwanathan, R., A. Iannaccone, T. M. Scott, S. B.
Kritchevsky, B. J. Jennings, G. Carboni, G. Forma, et al.
"Macular Pigment Optical Density is Related to Cognitive
Function in Older People." *Age and Ageing* 43, no. 2 (2014):
271–75. https://doi.org/10.1093/ageing/aft210.

Walk, Anne M., Caitlyn G. Edwards, Nicholas W.
Baumgartner, Morgan R. Chojnacki, Alicia R. Covello, Ginger
E. Reeser, Billy R. Hammond, et al. "The Role of Retinal
Carotenoids and Age on Neuroelectric Indices of Attentional
Control among Early to Middle-Aged Adults." *Frontiers in
Aging Neuroscience* 9 (2017).
https://doi.org/10.3389/fnagi.2017.00183.

Chapter 3

"Added Sugars." n.d. https://www.heart.org/en/healthy-
living/healthy-eating/eat-smart/sugar/added-sugars.

Barclay, Eliza. "Fruit Juice Vs. Soda? Both Beverages Pack in
Sugar, Health Risks." June 9, 2014.

https://www.npr.org/sections/thesalt/2014/06/09/31923076
5/fruit-juice-vs-soda-both-beverages-pack-in-sugar-and-
health-risk.

Baumeister, Roy F. "Research." Roy F. Baumeister. Accessed
September 11, 2018.
http://www.roybaumeister.com/research/#self-control.

Blackburn, Elizabeth H., and Elissa Epel. *The Telomere Effect:
A Revolutionary Approach to Living Younger, Healthier,
Longer*. New York: Grand Central Publishing, 2018.

"Cortisol – Its Role in Stress, Inflammation, and Indications
for Diet Therapy." Today's Dietitian. Accessed September 11,
2018.
http://www.todaysdietitian.com/newarchives/111609p38.sht
ml.

"Hand Portioning for Each Food Group," n.d.
https://www.ideafit.com/fitness-library/hand-portioning-for-
each-food-group.

Johnson, Rachel K., Lawrence J. Appel, Michael Brands,
Barbara V. Howard, Michael Lefevre, Robert H. Lustig, Frank
Sacks, Lyn M. Steffen, and Judith Wylie-Rosett. "Dietary
Sugars Intake and Cardiovascular Health." *Circulation* 120,
no. 11 (2009): 1011–20.
https://doi.org/10.1161/circulationaha.109.192627.

Maki, K. C., A. K. Phillips-Eakley, and K. N. Smith. "The
Effects of Breakfast Consumption and Composition on
Metabolic Wellness with a Focus on Carbohydrate
Metabolism." *Advances in Nutrition: An International Review
Journal* 7, no. 3 (2016).
https://doi.org/10.3945/an.115.010314.

Poggiogalle, Eleonora, Humaira Jamshed, and Courtney M. Peterson. "Circadian Regulation of Glucose, Lipid, and Energy Metabolism in Humans." *Metabolism* 84 (2018): 11–27. https://doi.org/10.1016/j.metabol.2017.11.017.

Rock, David. *Your Brain at Work: Strategies for Overcoming Distraction, Regaining Focus, and Working Smarter All Day Long*. New York, USA: HarperCollins, 2009.

"Welcome to the USDA Food Composition Databases." USDA Food Composition Databases, n.d. https://ndb.nal.usda.gov/ndb/.

Chapter 4
American Heart Association. "Whole Grains, Refined Grains, and Dietary Fiber." n.d. http://www.heart.org/HEARTORG/GettingHealthy/Nutrition Center/HealthyDietGoals/Whole-Grains-and-Fiber_UCM_303249_Article.jsp.

Baumeister, Roy. "Research." n.d. http://www.roybaumeister.com/research/#self-control.

Bisschop, P. H., H. P. Sauerwein, E. Endert, and J. A. Romijn. "Isocaloric Carbohydrate Deprivation Induces Protein Catabolism despite a Low T3-Syndrome in Healthy Men." *Clinical Endocrinology* 54, no. 1 (2001): 75–80. https://doi.org/10.1046/j.1365-2265.2001.01158.x.

Brinkworth, Grant D. "Long-Term Effects of a Very Low-Carbohydrate Diet and a Low-Fat Diet on Mood and Cognitive Function." *Archives of Internal Medicine* 169, no. 20 (September 2009): 1873.

https://doi.org/10.1001/archinternmed.2009.329.

Center for Food Safety and Applied Nutrition. "Overview of Food Ingredients, Additives & Colors." U.S. Food and Drug Administration. FDA, n.d. https://www.fda.gov/food/food-ingredients-packaging/overview-food-ingredients-additives-colors.

DesMaisons, Kathleen. *Potatoes Not Prozac: Simple Solutions for Sugar Addiction*. New York: Simon & Schuster Paperbacks, 2019.

Fernández-Elías, Valentín E., Juan F. Ortega, Rachael K. Nelson, and Ricardo Mora-Rodriguez. "Relationship between Muscle Water and Glycogen Recovery after Prolonged Exercise in the Heat in Humans." *European Journal of Applied Physiology* 115, no. 9 (2015): 1919–26. https://doi.org/10.1007/s00421-015-3175-z.

FNP, Kathleen Davis. "Sleep Deprivation: Causes, Symptoms, and Treatment." January 25, 2018. https://www.medicalnewstoday.com/articles/307334.php.

Gabel, Luci. "Losing Weight Fast – Two Athletes Tell All. April 9, 2017. https://lucifit.com/losing-weight-fast-two-athletes-tell-all/.

Gabel, Luci. "How 10,000 People Lost Weight and Continue to Keep it Off." September 24, 2016. https://lucifit.com/10000-people-lost-weight-continue-keep-off/.

Kose, Engin, Orkide Guzel, Korcan Demir, and Nur Arslan. "Changes of Thyroid Hormonal Status in Patients Receiving Ketogenic Diet Due to Intractable Epilepsy." *Journal of*

Pediatric Endocrinology and Metabolism 30, no. 4 (January 2017). https://doi.org/10.1515/jpem-2016-0281.

Lane, Amy R., Joseph W. Duke, and Anthony C. Hackney. "Influence of Dietary Carbohydrate Intake on the Free Testosterone: Cortisol Ratio Responses to Short-Term Intensive Exercise Training." *European Journal of Applied Physiology* 108, no. 6 (2009): 1125–31. https://doi.org/10.1007/s00421-009-1220-5.

Lemaire, Jane B, Jean E Wallace, Kelly Dinsmore, Adriane M Lewin, William A Ghali, and Delia Roberts. "Physician Nutrition and Cognition during Work Hours: Effect of a Nutrition Based Intervention," August 17, 2010. https://bmchealthservres.biomedcentral.com/articles/10.1186 /1472-6963-10-241.

Mayer, Emeran A. *The Mind-Gut Connection: How the Hidden Conversation within Our Bodies Impacts Our Mood, Our Choices, and Our Overall Health*. New York: Harper Collins, 2016.

Mosconi, Lisa. *Brain Food: The Surprising Science of Eating for Cognitive Power*. New York: Avery, an imprint of Penguin Random House, 2018.

National Heart Lung and Blood Institute, and U.S. Department of Health and Human Services. "Sleep Deprivation and Deficiency." n.d. http://www.nhlbi.nih.gov/health-topics/sleep-deprivation-and-deficiency.

National Potato Council. "2019 NPC Statistical Yearbook," 2019.

https://www.nationalpotatocouncil.org/files/5015/6380/8213/2019_Stat_Book__fnl.pdf

Philippou, Elena, and Marios Constantinou. "The Influence of Glycemic Index on Cognitive Functioning: A Systematic Review of the Evidence." *Advances in Nutrition* 5, no. 2 (June 2014): 119–30. https://doi.org/10.3945/an.113.004960.

Serog, P, M Apfelbaum, N Autissier, F Baigts, L Brigant, and A Ktorza. "Effects of Slimming and Composition of Diets on VO2 and Thyroid Hormones in Healthy Subjects." *The American Journal of Clinical Nutrition* 35, no. 1 (January 1982): 24–35. https://doi.org/10.1093/ajcn/35.1.24.

St. Pierre, Brian. "Carb Controversy: Why Low-Carb Diets Have Got It All Wrong." Precision Nutrition, February 19, 2018. https://www.precisionnutrition.com/low-carb-diets.

Walker, Matthew P. *Why We Sleep: Unlocking the Power of Sleep and Dreams*. New York, NY: Scribner, an imprint of Simon & Schuster, Inc., 2018.

Wood, Patrick B. "Role of Central Dopamine in Pain and Analgesia." *Expert Review of Neurotherapeutics* 8, no. 5 (2008): 781–97. https://doi.org/10.1586/14737175.8.5.781.

Writer, Endocrinology Advisor Contributing. "Cause or Effect? The Link Between Psychological Stress and Osteoporosis." June 6, 2019. https://www.endocrinologyadvisor.com/home/topics/bone-metabolism/cause-or-effect-the-link-between-psychological-stress-and-osteoporosis/2/.

Zimmer, Carl. "Fiber Is Good for You. Now Scientists May Know Why." January 1, 2018.

https://www.nytimes.com/2018/01/01/science/food-fiber-microbiome-inflammation.html.

Zou, Jun, Benoit Chassaing, Vishal Singh, Michael Pellizzon, Matthew Ricci, Michael D. Fythe, Matam Vijay Kumar, and Andrew T. Gewirtz. "Fiber-Mediated Nourishment of Gut Microbiota Protects against Diet-Induced Obesity by Restoring IL-22-Mediated Colonic Health." *Cell Host & Microbe* 23, no. 1 (2018).
https://doi.org/10.1016/j.chom.2017.11.003.

Chapter 5
"All about the Protein Foods Group." Choose MyPlate. August 10, 2018. https://www.choosemyplate.gov/protein-foods.

Bouvard, Véronique, Dana Loomis, Kathryn Z Guyton, Yann Grosse, Fatiha El Ghissassi, Lamia Benbrahim-Tallaa, Neela Guha, Heidi Mattock, and Kurt Straif. "Carcinogenicity of Consumption of Red and Processed Meat." *The Lancet Oncology* 16, no. 16 (2015): 1599–1600.
https://doi.org/10.1016/s1470-2045(15)00444-1.

"Calcium/Vitamin D Requirements, Recommended Foods & Supplements." National Osteoporosis Foundation.
https://www.nof.org/patients/treatment/calciumvitamin-d/.

Cataldo, Donna, and Matthew Blair. "Protein Intake for Optimal Muscle Maintenance." *Protein Intake for Optimal Muscle Maintenance*. American College of Sports Medicine, 2015.

Center for Food Safety and Applied Nutrition. "Nutrition Information for Raw Vegetables." December 2017.

https://www.fda.gov/food/food-labeling-nutrition/nutrition-information-raw-vegetables.

Examine.com and Kamal Patel. "Should one gram per pound be the new RDA for bodybuilders?" Last updated February 12, 2020. https://examine.com/nutrition/should-one-gram-per-pound-be-the-new-rda-for-bodybuilders/.

Examine.com and Alex Leaf. "How much protein do you need per day?" Last updated February 12, 2020. https://examine.com/nutrition/how-much-protein-do-you-need/.

"Goat Milk: Is It Really Healthier Than Cow's Milk?" December 14, 2018. https://www.nutritionadvance.com/goat-milk-vs-cow-milk/.

Ivy, John L., and Lisa M. Ferguson-Stegall. "Nutrient Timing." *American Journal of Lifestyle Medicine* 8, no. 4 (2013): 246–59. https://doi.org/10.1177/1559827613502444.

Jianqin, Sun, Xu Leiming, Xia Lu, Gregory W. Yelland, Jiayi Ni, and Andrew Clarke. "Effects of Milk Containing Only A2 Beta Casein versus Milk Containing Both A1 and A2 Beta Casein Proteins on Gastrointestinal Physiology, Symptoms of Discomfort, and Cognitive Behavior of People with Self-Reported Intolerance to Traditional Cows' Milk." *Nutrition Journal* 15, no. 1 (2015). https://doi.org/10.1186/s12937-016-0164-y.

Lieberman, Harris R, Sanjiv Agarwal, and Victor L Fulgoni. "Tryptophan Intake in the US Adult Population Is Not Related to Liver or Kidney Function but Is Associated with Depression and Sleep Outcomes." *The Journal of Nutrition* 146, no. 12 (2016). https://doi.org/10.3945/jn.115.226969.

Mayer, Emeran A. *The Mind-Gut Connection: How the Hidden Conversation within Our Bodies Impacts Our Mood, Our Choices, and Our Overall Health*. New York: Harper Collins, 2016.

McNeill, Shalene, Phil Lofgren, and Mary Van Elswyk. "The Role of Lean Beef in Healthful Dietary Patterns." *Nutrition Today* 48, no. 4 (2013): 181–88. https://doi.org/10.1097/nt.0b013e31823db387.

Micha, Renata, Sarah K. Wallace, and Dariush Mozaffarian. "Red and Processed Meat Consumption and Risk of Incident Coronary Heart Disease, Stroke, and Diabetes Mellitus." *Circulation* 121, no. 21 (2010): 2271–83. https://doi.org/10.1161/circulationaha.109.924977.

Mosconi, Lisa. *Brain Food: The Surprising Science of Eating for Cognitive Power*. Avery, an Imprint of Penguin Random House, 2018.

National Institutes of Health. "Office of Dietary Supplements – Calcium." n.d. https://ods.od.nih.gov/factsheets/Calcium-HealthProfessional/.

National Institutes of Health. "Office of Dietary Supplements – Zinc." n.d. https://ods.od.nih.gov/factsheets/Zinc-Consumer/.

National Institutes of Health. "Office of Dietary Supplements – Folate." n.d. https://ods.od.nih.gov/factsheets/Folate-Consumer/.

National Institutes of Health. "Office of Dietary Supplements – Niacin." n.d. https://ods.od.nih.gov/factsheets/Niacin-Consumer/.

National Institutes of Health. "Office of Dietary Supplements - Vitamin B12." n.d. https://ods.od.nih.gov/factsheets/VitaminB12-Consumer/.

National Institutes of Health. "Office of Dietary Supplements - Vitamin B." n.d. https://ods.od.nih.gov/factsheets/VitaminB6-Consumer/.

"Nutrition Information and Statistics." n.d. https://nutritiondata.self.com/.

Ormsbee, Mike, Ph.D. "Protein Myths vs Facts." American College of Sports Medicine. YouTube, October 18, 2018. https://www.youtube.com/watch?v=s3VK84khZow.

"American College of Sports Medicine." *American College of Sports Medicine*, 2015. https://www.acsm.org/docs/default-source/files-for-resource-library/protein-intake-for-optimal-muscle-maintenance.pdf?sfvrsn=688d8896_2.

"Red Meat and Health." *Nutrition Today* 52, no. 4 (July/August 2017): 167-73. doi:10.1097/nt.0000000000000227.

Rohrmann, Sabine, and Jakob Linseisen. "Processed Meat: The Real Villain?" *Proceedings of the Nutrition Society* 75, no. 3 (January 2015): 233-41. https://doi.org/10.1017/s0029665115004255.

Szent-Györgyi, A.G. "Calcium Regulation of Muscle Contraction." *Biophysical Journal* 15, no. 7 (1975): 707-23. doi:10.1016/s0006-3495(75)85849-8.

Vitellio, Paola, Giuseppe Celano, Leonilde Bonfrate, Marco Gobbetti, Piero Portincasa, and Maria DeAngelis. "Effects of Bifidobacterium Longum and Lactobacillus Rhamnosus on Gut Microbiota in Patients with Lactose Intolerance and Persisting Functional Gastrointestinal Symptoms: A Randomised, Double-Blind, Cross-Over Study." *Nutrients* 11, no. 4 (2019): 886. https://doi.org/10.3390/nu11040886.

Wolk, A. "Potential Health Hazards of Eating Red Meat." *Journal of Internal Medicine* 281, no. 2 (June 2016): 106–22. https://doi.org/10.1111/joim.12543.

World Health Organization. "Q&A on the Carcinogenicity of the Consumption of Red Meat and Processed Meat." May 17, 2016. https://www.who.int/features/qa/cancer-red-meat/en/.

Chapter 6

Ketz, John Samuel, Mary C. Rodavich, and Kimberly M Barnes. "Absorption of Marine vs Non-Marine Sources of EPA and DHA." *FASEB*, 2013. https://www.fasebj.org/doi/10.1096/fasebj.27.1_supplement.867.3.

American Heart Association. "Fish and Omega-3 Fatty Acids." n.d. https://www.heart.org/en/healthy-living/healthy-eating/eat-smart/fats/fish-and-omega-3-fatty-acids.

American Heart Association. "*Trans* Fats," 2015.
https://www.heart.org/en/healthy-living/healthy-eating/eat-smart/fats/trans-fat.

American Heart Association. "Saturated Fats: Why All the Hubbub over Coconuts?" June 2017.
https://www.heart.org/en/news/2018/05/01/saturated-fats-why-all-the-hubbub-over-coconuts.

Blackburn, Elizabeth H., and Elissa Epel. *The Telomere Effect: A Revolutionary Approach to Living Younger, Healthier, Longer*. New York: Grand Central Publishing, 2018.

Center for Science in the Public Interest. "Four Coconut Oil Myths and the Facts You Should Know." June 2015.
https://cspinet.org/tip/four-coconut-oil-myths-and-facts-you-should-know.

Center for Science in the Public Interest. "Coconut Oil Myths Persist in Face of the Facts," June 2016.
https://cspinet.org/tip/coconut-oil-myths-persist-face-facts.

"Cholecystokinin." Accessed 2019.
http://www.yourhormones.info/.

Cladis, Dennis P., Alison C. Kleiner, Helene H. Freiser, and Charles R. Santerre. "Fatty Acid Profiles of Commercially Available Finfish Fillets in the United States." *Lipids* 49, no. 10 (2014): 1005–18. https://doi.org/10.1007/s11745-014-3932-5.

Corliss, Julie. "Finding Omega-3 Fats in Fish: Farmed versus Wild." December 22, 2015.
https://www.health.harvard.edu/blog/finding-omega-3-fats-in-fish-farmed-versus-wild-201512238909.

Croll, Pauline H., Trudy Voortman, M. Arfan Ikram, Oscar H. Franco, Josje D. Schoufour, Daniel Bos, and Meike W. Vernooij. "Better Diet Quality Relates to Larger Brain Tissue Volumes." *Neurology* 90, no. 24 (2018). https://doi.org/10.1212/wnl.0000000000005691.

Eltagouri, Marwa. "Report Claims Sugar Industry Hid Connection to Heart Disease for Decades." November 22, 2017.https://www.washingtonpost.com/news/wonk/wp/201 7/11/22/report-claims-sugar-industry-hid-connection-to-heart-disease-for-decades/.

European Food Safety Authority (EFSA), Parma, Italy. "Scientific Opinion on Dietary Reference Values for Water." *EFSA Journal* 8, no. 3 (2010). https://doi.org/10.2903/j.efsa.2010.1459.

"Fact: Not All Omega-3s Are Created Equal." n.d. https://alwaysomega3s.com/learn/epa-dha-ala-omega-3s.

"Fish and Omega-3 Fatty Acids." n.d. https://www.heart.org/HEARTORG/General/Fish-and-Omega-3-Fatty-Acids_UCM_303248_Article.jsp.

Gardner, Christopher D., John F. Trepanowski, Liana C. Del Gobbo, Michelle E. Hauser, Joseph Rigdon, John P. A. Ioannidis, Manisha Desai, and Abby C. King. "Effect of Low-Fat vs Low-Carbohydrate Diet on 12-Month Weight Loss in Overweight Adults and the Association with Genotype Pattern or Insulin Secretion." *Jama* 319, no. 7 (2018): 667. https://doi.org/10.1001/jama.2018.0245.

Khaw, Kay-Tee, Stephen J Sharp, Leila Finikarides, Islam Afzal, Marleen Lentjes, Robert Luben, and Nita G Forouhi. "Randomised Trial of Coconut Oil, Olive Oil or Butter on

Blood Lipids and Other Cardiovascular Risk Factors in Healthy Men and Women." *BMJ Open* 8, no. 3 (2018). https://doi.org/10.1136/bmjopen-2017-020167.

Mayer, Emeran A. *The Mind-Gut Connection: How the Hidden Conversation within Our Bodies Impacts Our Mood, Our Choices, and Our Overall Health*. New York: Harper Collins, 2016.

Morris, Martha Clare, Denis A. Evans, Julia L. Bienias, Christine C. Tangney, David A. Bennett, Neelum Aggarwal, Julie Schneider, and Robert S. Wilson. "Dietary Fats and the Risk of Incident Alzheimer Disease." *Archives of Neurology* 60, no. 2 (2003): 194. https://doi.org/10.1001/archneur.60.2.194.

Morris, Martha, MD Clare. *Diet for the MIND: The Latest Science on What to Eat to Prevent Alzheimer's and Cognitive Decline*. New York, NY: Little, Brown and Company, 2017.

Mosconi, Lisa. *Brain Food: The Surprising Science of Eating for Cognitive Power*. New York: Avery, an imprint of Penguin Random House, 2018.

NIH. "Office of Dietary Supplements – Omega-3 Fatty Acids." n.d. https://ods.od.nih.gov/factsheets/Omega3FattyAcids-HealthProfessional/#.

"Nutrient Recommendations: Dietary Reference Intakes (DRI)." Accessed 2019. *https://ods.od.nih.gov/Health_Information/Dietary_Referenc e_Intakes.aspx.*

"Nutrition Information and Statistics," n.d. https://nutritiondata.self.com/.

"Omega-3 Fatty Acids Facts," 2019.
https://www.webmd.com/healthy-aging/omega-3-fatty-acids-fact-sheet#1.

Popkin, Barry M., D'Anci, Kristen E., and Rosenberg, Irwin H. "Water, Hydration, and Health." *Nutrition Reviews* 68, no. 8 (2010): 439–58. https://dx.doi.org/10.1111%2Fj.1753-4887.2010.00304.x

Precision Nutrition. "The Ketogenic Diet: Does it live up to the hype: The pros, the cons, and the facts about this not-so-new diet craze." April 5, 2018. https://www.precisionnutrition.com/ketogenic-diet.

Severson, Tracy, RD, LD, Sergio, Fazio, MD, PhD. Oregon Health & Science University. "Trimming the Fat on Diet Recommendations for a Healthy Heart: Emphasis on Eating Patterns over Dietary Restrictions." June 15, 2017. http://professional.heart.org/professional/ScienceNews/UCM_494505_Trimming-the-Fat-on-Diet-Recommendations-for-a-Healthy-Heart-Emphasis-on-Eating.jsp.

St-Onge, Marie-Pierre, Aubrey Bosarge, Laura Lee T. Goree, and Betty Darnell. "Medium Chain Triglyceride Oil Consumption as Part of a Weight Loss Diet Does Not Lead to an Adverse Metabolic Profile When Compared to Olive Oil." *Journal of the American College of Nutrition* 27, no. 5 (2008): 547–52. https://doi.org/10.1080/07315724.2008.10719737.

Streitbürger, Daniel-Paolo, Harald E. Möller, Marc Tittgemeyer, Margret Hund-Georgiadis, Matthias L. Schroeter, and Karsten Mueller. "Investigating Structural Brain Changes of Dehydration Using Voxel-Based Morphometry." August 29, 2012.

https://journals.plos.org/plosone/article?id=10.1371/journal.pone.0044195.

USDA. "Dietary Guidelines for Americans 2015-2020 Eight Edition." n.d. https://health.gov/dietaryguidelines/2015/.

Zaffron, Steve, and Dave Logan. *The Three Laws of Performance Rewriting the Future of Your Organization and Your Life*. San Francisco: Jossey-Bass, 2009.

Chapter 7
Blackburn, Elizabeth H., and Elissa Epel. *The Telomere Effect: A Revolutionary Approach to Living Younger, Healthier, Longer*. New York: Grand Central Publishing, 2018.

Corbyn, Zoë. "Elizabeth Blackburn on the Telomere Effect: 'It's about Keeping Healthier for Longer.'" January 29, 2017. https://www.theguardian.com/science/2017/jan/29/telomere-effect-elizabeth-blackburn-nobel-prize-medicine-chromosomes.

Mayer, Emeran A. *The Mind-Gut Connection: How the Hidden Conversation within Our Bodies Impacts Our Mood, Our Choices, and Our Overall Health*. New York: Harper Collins, 2016.

| ADDITIONAL GOOD READS |

The following articles weren't used as references but can provide you with additional details on certain topics in each chapter. These as well as some of the books and articles in the References section will help you take a deeper dive into the topics of this book that you're interested in.

Chapter 1
"Beware of the Health Halo," n.d. http://www.berkeleywellness.com/healthy-eating/food/article/health-food-beware-halo-effect.

Chapter 2
Dennett, Carrie. "Celery Juice Will Not Work Miracles, No Matter What You Read on Goop," February 25, 2019. https://www.washingtonpost.com/lifestyle/wellness/celery-juice-will-not-work-miracles-no-matter-what-you-read-on-goop/2019/02/22/a4ddac18-348f-11e9-af5b-b51b7ff322e9_story.html.

Harvard Health Publishing. "Add Color to Your Diet for Good Nutrition," n.d. https://www.health.harvard.edu/staying-healthy/add-color-to-your-diet-for-good-nutrition.

Chapter 3
Gabel, Luci. "What's for Breakfast?" LuciFit. Accessed September 11, 2018. http://lucifit.com/whats-for-breakfast/.

Gabel, Luci. "Putting What We Currently Know About Sugar into Perspective." LuciFit, March 21, 2017. https://lucifit.com/putting-what-we-currently-know-about-sugar-into-perspective/.

Chapter 4
American Diabetes Association. "Checking Your Blood Glucose," August 2018. http://www.diabetes.org/living-with-diabetes/treatment-and-care/blood-glucose-control/checking-your-blood-glucose.html.

Friedman, Noah. "A Sleep Expert Explains What Happens to Your Body and Brain If You Don't Get Enough Sleep," March 14, 2019. https://www.businessinsider.com/what-happens-when-you-dont-get-enough-sleep-2017-12.

Gabel, Luci. "Your Hidden Fitness," November 5, 2018. https://lucifit.com/your-hidden-fitness/.

Peri, Camille. "10 Surprising Effects of Lack of Sleep," n.d. https://www.webmd.com/sleep-disorders/features/10-results-sleep-loss.

WebMD. "Blood Sugar Levels: How Glucose Levels Affect Your Body," n.d. http://www.webmd.com/diabetes/how-sugar-affects-diabetes.

Chapter 5
Binnie, Mary Ann, Karine Barlow, Valerie Johnson, and Carol Harrison. "Red Meats: Time for a Paradigm Shift in Dietary Advice." *Meat Science* 98, no. 3 (2014): 445–51. https://doi.org/10.1016/j.meatsci.2014.06.024.

Grieger, Lynn. "Is Lunch Meat Healthy?" December 9, 2016. https://www.rise.us/is-lunch-meat-healthy/.

Chapter 6
Gabel, Luci. "Just How Dangerous Is Sitting?" June 16, 2017. https://lucifit.com/how-dangerous-sitting/.

Gabel, Luci. "Omega-3: What Is It? Why Do We Need It? Where Do You Get It?" September 29, 2017. https://lucifit.com/omega-3s-in-what/.

Gabel, Luci. "If Low-Fat V.S. Low-Carb Diet Doesn't Matter for Weight Loss, What Does?" June 4, 2019. https://lucifit.com/low-fat-v-s-low-carb-diet-doesnt-matter-weight-loss-what-does/.

"Grass-Fed Beef for Omega-3s?" Accessed August 2017. http://www.berkeleywellness.com/healthy-eating/food/nutrition/article/grass-fed-beef-omega-3s.

Hannaford, Alex. "The Bulletproof Diet: Simplistic, Invalid and Unscientific," July 8, 2015. https://www.telegraph.co.uk/books/what-to-read/the-bulletproof-diet-simplistic-invalid-and-unscientific/.

Harvard Health Publishing. "Taking Aim at Belly Fat." Accessed 2019. https://www.health.harvard.edu/staying-healthy/taking-aim-at-belly-fat.

Zimmer, Carl. "Fiber Is Good for You. Now Scientists May Know Why." January 1, 2018. *https://www.nytimes.com/2018/01/01/science/food-fiber-microbiome-inflammation.html.*

ACKNOWLEDGMENTS

I owe thanks to so many people who have supported me in bringing this book together. I have endless gratitude to my perfect husband, Denis Trofimov, for forever being supportive and always believing in me, for taking the back seat to this book on so many weekends and holidays when I needed to buckle down and write, and for always having a smile to offer when I finally emerged from the office. Thanks to Robin Tucker for being my angel of constant encouragement to become all that I'm meant to be. To Sandra Hughes, for helping me to confidently integrate my life's work into this book. To my dad and his wife, Liz, for consistently encouraging me and for the day you took me out for coffee and finally convinced me to start writing a book. To Ginny Marcin, the first writer in my family, for introducing me to good writing standards so many years ago. To Claudia Gabel, the second writer in my family for words of encouragement and grounding when I needed it. To Veronica Cruz and The Downtown Yoga Shala in San Jose, and my friends, family, and clients who preordered this book and believed in it—and me—long before it was finished. To Lee Constantine at Publishizer.com, who gave me the push I needed to get a publisher. To Wendy Hall, my secret weapon of an editor who makes me feel no less than Wonder Woman. To my publisher, Nick Courtright at Atmosphere Press, for consistent patience and positivity in helping me get through the long and windy road that was the creation of my first book. And to you, my reader, for picking this book up and giving it a read. My hope and goal is that you reap many rewards from it.

ABOUT ATMOSPHERE PRESS

Atmosphere Press is an independent, full-service publisher for excellent books in all genres and for all audiences. Learn more about what we do at atmospherepress.com.

We encourage you to check out some of Atmosphere's latest releases, which are available at Amazon.com and via order from your local bookstore:

Disruption Games: How to Thrive on Serial Failure, nonfiction by Trond Undheim
Itsuki, a novel by Zach MacDonald
A Surprising Measure of Subliminal Sadness, short stories by Sue Powers
Eyeless Mind, nonfiction by Stephanie Duesing
Saint Lazarus Day, short stories by R. Conrad Speer
My Father's Eyes, a novel by Michael Osborne
The Lower Canyons, a novel by John Manuel
A Blameless Walk, nonfiction by Charles Hopkins
The Horror of 1888, nonfiction by Betty Plombon
Shiftless, a novel by Anthony C. Murphy
White Snake Diary, nonfiction by Jane P. Perry
From Rags to Rags, essays by Ellie Guzman
The Escapist, a novel by Karahn Washington
A Cage Called Freedom, a novel by Paul P.S. Berg
Giving Up the Ghost, essays by Tina Cabrera
Family Legends, Family Lies, nonfiction by Wendy Hoke
Shining in Infinity, a novel by Charles McIntyre
Buildings Without Murders, a novel by Dan Gutstein

ABOUT THE AUTHOR

Luci Gabel, MBA, MA, ACE, ACSM is a Leadership Optimal Performance Coach. Along with experience and multiple advanced degrees in business, nutrition, and physiology, she's held leadership roles in the Department of Defense and private companies, and has been an entrepreneur and start-up founder. Luci has lived and worked in Seoul, South Korea; New York City, Washington, DC; Honolulu, Hawaii; and Silicon Valley. A former triathlon competitor, blackbelt in Taekwondo, and enthusiast of all kinds of workouts, she likes to be where there is plenty of urban excitement, and where outdoor activities and healthy food is easy to find. She currently lives in Los Angeles with her husband.